Bond

No.1 for exam success

Verbal Reasoning

10 Minute Tests

10–11+ years

OXFORD
UNIVERSITY PRESS

TEST 1: **Similars and Opposites**

Test time: 0 5 10 minutes

Underline the two words, one from each group, which are the most opposite in meaning.

Example	(dawn, <u>early</u>, wake)	(<u>late</u>, stop, sunrise)
1	(tidy, dust, clean)	(neat, scruffy, brush)
2	(climb, broad, slender)	(narrow, wide, high)
3	(hearty, cough, unwell)	(strong, cold, healthy)
4	(pale, red, coloured)	(flushed, faint, whiten)

Find a word that is similar in meaning to the word in capital letters and that rhymes with the second word.

Example	CABLE	tyre	wire
5	DEFEND	detect	____________
6	SLICE	fleece	____________
7	KNOT	sigh	____________
8	MINUTE	shiny	____________

Underline the pair of words most opposite in meaning.

Example	cup, mug	coffee, milk	<u>hot, cold</u>
9	few, many	some, any	lift, raise
10	silly, foolish	stupid, sensible	serious, kind
11	show, display	conceal, hide	present, absent
12	far, near	distant, horizon	planet, star

Underline the word in brackets closest in meaning to the word in capitals.

Example	UNHAPPY	(unkind, death, laughter, <u>sad</u>, friendly)
13	QUIET	(almost, noisy, busy, silence, thought)
14	CLASS	(children, work, school, student, group)
15	TEAR	(shred, drop, cries, sad, prick)
16	QUERY	(answer, question, peculiar, same, reply)

Look at the pair of words on the left. Underline the one word in the brackets that goes with the word outside the brackets in the same way as the first two words go together.

Example	good, better	bad, (naughty, worst, <u>worse</u>, nasty)
17	upset, cry	happy, (pleased, sad, growl, laugh)
18	left, right	for, (five, with, against, hand)
19	finger, wrist	toe, (foot, ankle, leg, nail)
20	reveal, show	retain, (return, get, stop, keep)

Total

TEST 2: **Sorting Words**

Test time: 0 5 10 minutes

Underline the one word in brackets which will go equally well with both the pairs of words outside the brackets.

Example	rush, attack	cost, fee	(price, hasten, strike, <u>charge</u>, money)
1	talon, pincer	scratch, tear	(rake, nail, foot, claw)
2	even, flat	position, stage	(level, dull, horizontal, period)
3	pour, empty out	end, furthest point	(overbalance, apex, tip, fall)
4	site, situation	put, allocate	(location, place, circumstance, move)
5	clean, clear	innocent, virtuous	(pure, not guilty, harmless, hygienic)

Rearrange the muddled words in capital letters in the following sentences so that they make sense.

Example There are sixty SNODCES seconds in a UTMINE minute.

6 She put the picnic KSATEB ________ on the CHKTINE ________ table.

7 It is cold DSIOUET ________ so put your KJATCE ________ on.

8 Straight after our SHILENG ________ SNOLES ________, we had French.

9 Our local BRALIYR ________ has a RAVIDE ________ selection of books.

10 In the OLOHSC ________ holidays, we went PNIGMCA ________ in Wales.

Rearrange the letters in capitals to make another word. The new word has something to do with the first two words or phrases.

Example	spot	soil	SAINT	STAIN
11	prickle	splinter	NORTH	________
12	clutch	grip	SCALP	________
13	cry	complaint	TABLE	________
14	beat	pulse	BROTH	________
15	jeans	material	MINED	________

Find and underline the two words that need to change places for each sentence to make sense.

Example She went to <u>letter</u> the <u>write</u>.

16 The door sign has fallen off the toilet.

17 You have arrived time in just for tea.

18 Why have you put your feet on the wrong shoes?

19 In a park, the storm bench was blown over.

20 The autumn fall during the leaves.

Total

Test 3: Selecting Words

Test time: 0 5 10 minutes

Which one letter can be added to the front of all of these words to make new words?

Example c̲are c̲at c̲rate c̲all c̲lip

1 __age __ally __at __oar __each

2 __ice __an __alley __omit __ow

3 __hunk __lash __hip __rush __raft

4 __ash __align __utter __eat __ail

Find two letters that will end the first word and start the second word.

Example pas (t a) ste

5 squ (__ __) ea

6 spa (__ __) ally

7 twi (__ __) op

8 bo (__ __) orn

Underline two words, one from each group, that go together to form a new word. The word in the first group always comes first.

Example (hand, green, for) (light, house, sure)

9 (fourth, pass, trouble) (with, some, by)

10 (in, out, on) (too, shirt, vest)

11 (bear, bore, be) (ring, gun, for)

12 (for, end, first) (rest, less, tale)

Underline the word in brackets that goes best with the words given outside the brackets.

Example word, paragraph, sentence (pen, cap, letter, top, stop)

13 road, street, avenue (town, lane, footpath, car, walk)

14 toes, ankle, heel (son, hand, stocking, foot, wrist)

15 ruler, rubber, pencil (lesson, case, pen, book, school)

16 sandal, slipper, boot (socks, glove, person, hat, trainer)

Underline the one word in each group that can be made from the letters of the word in capital letters.

Example CHAMPION camping notch peach cramp chimp

17 PARTICLE patch crate prick letter treat

18 MONSTER mower stare stone moist stream

19 COUPLES place supple plush scoop slope

20 FLOUNDER drown folder friend drain floor

Total

TEST 4: **Finding Words**

Test time: 0 5 10 minutes

Write the four-letter word hidden at the end of one word and the beginning of the next word. The order of the letters may not be changed.

Example We had bat<u>s and</u> balls. sand

1 A long icicle appeared on her windowsill last night. ____________

2 The ghostly sound of both owls could be heard. ____________

3 My cousins have stones all around their pond. ____________

4 In an airport lounge any unattended parcel looks suspicious. ____________

5 Pour the cream into the striped jug please. ____________

Find the three-letter word that can be added to the letters in capitals to make a new word. The new word will complete the sentence sensibly. Write the three-letter word.

Example The cat sprang onto the MO. USE

6 In our pond we have a WR feature. ____________

7 Maisy's VAGE has pretty thatched cottages. ____________

8 There is a zebra CROSG right by our school. ____________

9 Toby's rabbit is white with red E. ____________

10 In class, we put up our hands before SKING. ____________

Find a word that can be put in front of each of the following words to make a new, compound word.

Example cast fall ward pour down

11	market	model	natural	star	______
12	thing	how	what	body	______
13	witness	shadow	brow	ball	______
14	drop	coat	forest	bow	______
15	guard	boat	style	time	______

Move one letter from the first word to the second word to make two new words.

Example hunt sip hut snip

16	bread	tint	____________	____________
17	bung	amble	____________	____________
18	want	pin	____________	____________
19	bridle	growing	____________	____________
20	whine	heart	____________	____________

Total

TEST 5: **Alphabetical Order and Substitution**

Test time: 0 5 10 minutes

If these words were put into alphabetical order, which word would come third?

1	called	curries	charge	colour	circle	________
2	quaver	quarry	quilts	queen	quartz	________
3	dragon	dreams	drowsy	drench	drinks	________
4	planet	placed	palace	pandas	pillow	________
5	galaxy	gables	garden	gained	gallop	________

If p = 10, q = 4, r = 3, s = 6, t = 2 and u = 24, find the value of the following.

6 $(p + r) - s =$ ________

7 $ps =$ ________

8 $(\frac{u}{q}) \times s =$ ________

9 $(u - p) + (s - q) =$ ________

Using the same values as above, write the answers as letters.

10 $(u - q) - p =$ ________

11 $qrt =$ ________

12 $pr - s =$ ________

13 $q^2 - p =$ ________

14 $\frac{qs}{u} + t =$ ________

15 $\frac{s + u}{p} =$ ________

If A = 1, E = 2, L = 3, P = 4, S = 5 and T = 6, find the values of these words when the letters are added together.

16 PLEASE ________

17 PLEAT ________

18 LEAST ________

19 STAPLE ________

Using the same values as above, work out the value of this calculation.

20 LAPSE – PALE ________

Total

TEST 6: **Word Progressions**

Test time: 0 5 10 minutes

Look at the first group of three words. The word in the middle has been made from the two other words. Complete the second group of three words in the same way, making a new word in the middle of the group.

Example	PAIN	INTO	TOOK	ALSO	SOON	ONLY
1	GRIN	GRIP	PINK	PLUG	______	NAVE
2	TIME	MILK	LOOK	SLED	______	SORE
3	PAST	SPOT	TORN	ROTA	______	YAWN
4	DUMB	BULB	LOBE	LAWN	______	VEER

Change the first word into the last word by changing one letter at a time and making two new, different words in the middle.

Example	CASE	CASH	WASH	WISH
5	ZOOM	______	______	LOCK
6	TUBE	______	______	CARE
7	GOAT	______	______	BEAN
8	SORT	______	______	FIRM
9	DIET	______	______	PART
10	TIME	______	______	SAFE

Change the first word of the third pair in the same way as the other pairs to give a new word.

Example	bind, hind	bare, hare	but, hut
11	rage, role	page, pole	sage, ______
12	lead, loud	tear, tour	beat, ______
13	shaves, have	tablet, able	misled, ______
14	stream, team	chrome, home	stroll, ______

Find the missing number by using the two numbers outside the brackets in the same way as the other sets of numbers.

Example 2 [8] 4 3[18]6 5 [25] 5

15	7 [28] 4	6 [18] 3	9 [__] 5	**16**	4 [10] 1	3 [18] 6	5 [__] 7
17	7 [1] 7	6 [2] 3	12 [__] 4	**18**	5 [10] 4	3 [14] 8	2 [__] 6
19	4 [7] 3	9 [17] 8	11 [__] 6	**20**	6 [10] 2	5 [12] 3	2 [__] 1

Total

Test 7: **Logic**

Test time: 0 5 10 minutes

Tom had six lessons in different classrooms. Match the lessons he studied with the six unshaded rooms.

Tom studied English in a classroom with a lower number than the one he used for French.

History was in the classroom, directly across the corridor, opposite the classroom for Geography.

Maths was in between and next door to Geography and Science.

5	4	3	2 (shaded)	1
CORRIDOR				
10 (shaded)	9 (shaded)	8	7	6 (shaded)

1–6 Room 1 = ____________ Room 3 = ____________ Room 4 = ____________

Room 5 = ____________ Room 7 = ____________ Room 8 = ____________

From the information supplied, answer the questions.

An explorer was in a dilemma. He needed to travel to his camp.

Using the map, what would the explorer encounter:

7 south of the camp? ____________ **8** east of the camp? ____________

In which direction would the explorer have to start to go if he decided to:

9 go over the mountains towards the camp? ____________

10 go through the jungle towards the camp? ____________

11 go through the swamp towards the camp? ____________

Class 6S were collecting information to make a graph on the pets owned by the class.

Rabbits were owned by Darren, William, Sita, Jane and Phil.
Sita, Brett, Jane and Sven all had goldfish. All those who owned a goldfish also had a cat, except Sven. William and Darren also had a dog.
Sandy, William and Brett each had a gerbil. Phil and Sita had a tortoise.

12 How many types of pet are mentioned? ____________

13–14 What pets does Darren have? ____________ ____________

15 How many children are mentioned? ____________

16–17 Which two children only have one pet each? ____________ ____________

18 Who has a dog and a gerbil? ____________

19 Who has a cat and a gerbil? ____________

20 Who has the most pets? ____________

Total

TEST 8: **Simple Codes**

Test time: 0 5 10 minutes

The code for the word COMPUTER is 72384169. Encode each of these words using the same code.

1 TRUE ____________

2 RUMP ____________

Decode these words using the same code as above.

3 3296 ____________

4 8291 ____________

If the code for SPENT is ORJAZ, what word is:

5 AJOZ ____________

6 OZJR ____________

If the code for CALMER is $+x£–@, what would be the code for:

7 MALE ____________

8 RACE ____________

Match the right word to each code given below.
TEST MAST TAME STEM

9 4617 ____________

10 4734 ____________

11 3471 ____________

12 1634 ____________

Decode these words using the same code as above.

13 7634 ____________

14 1764 ____________

Here are the codes for four words.
9mQ% mX%3 3Xm9 %Qm9
Match the right code to each word.

15 TURN ____________

16 RATS ____________

17 STAR ____________

18 NUTS ____________

Encode these words using the same code as above.

19 STUNT ____________

20 SATURN ____________

Total

TEST 9: More Complicated Codes

Test time: 0 5 10 minutes

A B C D E F G H I J K L M N O P Q R S T U V W X Y Z

The word FOOTBALL is written in a code as GPPUCBMM. Using the same code:

1 encode the word SOCCER. ______________

2 decode HPBM. ______________

The word TYPE is written in code as VARG. Encode these words using the same code.

3 JAM ______________

4 ZEBRA ______________

The word FAST is written in code as CXPQ. Encode these words using the same code.

5 TABLE ______________

6 PINK ______________

Decode these words using the same code as above.

7 MXOQ ______________

8 GXAB ______________

The word BEAD is written in code as 2514. Encode these words using the same code.

9 FEED ______________

10 CAGE ______________

11 HEAD ______________

Decode these words using the same code as above.

12 6135 ______________ **13** 85475 ______________

14 If the code for RIGHT is WNLMY, what is the code for LEFT? ______________

The code for the word BLACK is eodfn. Using the same code, pick the correct codes for these words.

sodq odun edun sodb

15 BARK ______________ **16** PLAY ______________

17 LARK ______________ **18** PLAN ______________

Decode these words using the same code as above.

19 elug ______________ **20** iohz ______________

Time for a break! Go to Puzzle Page 42

Total

TEST 10: Sequences

Test time: 0 5 10 minutes

Complete the following sentences in the best way by choosing one word from each set of brackets.

Example Tall is to (tree, <u>short</u>, colour) as narrow is to (thin, white, <u>wide</u>).

1 Ostrich is to (egg, bird, Africa) as fly is to (insect, sky, soar).

2 Speak is to (talk, mouth, word) as pace is to (stripe, stride, stand).

3 Hilarious is to (miserable, funny, comforting) as tragic is to (alive, fantastic, sad).

A B C D E F G H I J K L M N O P Q R S T U V W X Y Z

Fill in the missing letters and numbers. The alphabet has been written out to help you.

Example AB is to CD as PQ is to RS.

4 PON is to MLK as JIH is to ______.

5 FD is to HF as JH is to ______.

6 Ah is to Dk as Gn is to ______.

7 Z11 is to X10 as V9 is to ______.

8 M12N is to O14p as Q16R is to ______.

9 aZ is to bY as cX is to ______.

10 AF is to CH as EJ is to ______.

A B C D E F G H I J K L M N O P Q R S T U V W X Y Z

Give the two missing groups of letters and numbers in the following sequences. The alphabet has been written out to help you.

Example	CQ	DP	EQ	FP	GQ	HP		
11	10	4	20	6	___	___		
12	Ab	Cd	Ef	Gh	___	___		
13	33	zz	22	yy	___	___		
14	15m	18p	21s	24v	___	___		
15	___	___	8	16	32	64		
16	6	___	12	8	___	12	24	16
17	___	2	4	___	6	8	8	16
18	a3Z	b5Y	___	___	e11V	f13U	g15T	h17S
19	___	___	16	15	20	18	24	21
20	3Z	___	6X	___	13V	18U	24T	31S

Total

Test time: 0 5 10 minutes

Look at these groups of words.

A	B	C	D	E
rugby	iron	eagle	scarlet	rain
netball	lead	penguin	orange	cloud

Choose the correct group for each of these words below. Write in the group letter.

1–5 steel ____ flamingo ____ hail ____

purple ____ azure ____ hockey ____

sun ____ seagull ____ platinum ____

football ____

Find two letters that will end the first word and start the second word.

Example pas (t a) ste

6 cla (__ __) oon

7 swiv (__ __) ect

8 sty (__ __) mon

9 varni (__ __) out

10 pan (__ __) icle

Remove one letter from the word in capital letters to leave a new word. The meaning of the new word is given in the clue.

Example AUNT an insect ANT

11 TABLE a story ________

12 CLIMB an arm or a leg ________

13 BRIDLE marries a groom ________

14 FOWL a night bird ________

15 STEEP a pace ________

Underline the two words that are the odd ones out in the following groups of words.

Example black <u>king</u> purple green <u>house</u>

16 boot door slipper car snowshoe

17 beetroot carrot peach apple clementine

18 bear camel salmon crocodile mouse

19 camera CD player radio tape recorder binoculars

20 forest lake orchard pond wood

Total

Test 12: Mixed

Test time: 0 5 10 minutes

Underline the two words, one from each group, that are the closest in meaning.

Example (race, shop, <u>start</u>) (finish, <u>begin</u>, end)

1 (appear, disappear, collapse) (vanish, rebuild, apply)

2 (competent, competitor, companion) (capable, enemy, canopy)

3 (blue, aquamarine, scarlet) (black, beige, crimson)

4 (scamper, run, skip) (hop, scurry, scrounge)

5 (rubbish, wasteful, skip) (dust, wasteland, uneconomical)

Write the four-letter word hidden at the end of one word and the beginning of the next word. The order of the letters may not be changed.

Example We had bat<u>s and</u> balls. sand

6 Please remember you must open each window slowly. ________

7 I avoided the girl who made me cry. ________

8 The rope bridge swung in the breeze. ________

9 Explorers make epic journeys across the globe. ________

10 Tom's ball dented the wing of his father's car. ________

From the information supplied, underline the one statement below it that must be true.

11 Butter is a dairy product. Dairy products are made from milk.

A Butter is made from milk. **C** Dairy products are yellow.

B Milk comes from cows. **D** Cheese is a dairy product.

Find the letter which will end the first word and start the second word.

Example peac (h) ome

12 buil (__) rown

13 stam (__) roud

14 twic (__) ndure

15 dais (__) earn

If A = 5, S = 4, T = 3, R = 2 and E = 1, find the values of the following words when the letters are added together.

16 RAT ________

17 EAR ________

18 STAR ________

19 REST ________

20 STARE ________

Total

Test 13: Mixed

Test time: 0 5 10 minutes

Here are the number codes for four words.
3256 3526 6225 5223
Match the right code to each word.

1 FROM ____________ **2** ROOF ____________

3 FORM ____________ **4** MOOR ____________

5 Using the same code, decode 5226 ____________

Write the four-letter word hidden at the end of one word and the beginning of the next word. The order of the letters may not be changed.

Example We had bat<u>s and</u> balls. sand

6 I was stung by a wasp in my garden. ____________

7 In the dusk the nightingales were singing. ____________

8 The team stays in cheap hotels to save money. ____________

9 The tide tugged at the tarred rope holding the anchor. ____________

10 Ben and his friends consumed three loaves of bread. ____________

Find a word that is similar in meaning to the word in capital letters and that rhymes with the second word.

Example CABLE tyre wire

11 DIVIDE hair ____________

12 TALK flat ____________

13 LABOUR spoil ____________

14 ASCEND rhyme ____________

15 SOIL mirth ____________

Change the first word into the last word by changing one letter at a time, and making two new, different words in the middle.

Example CASE CASH WASH WISH

16 FLIT ____________ ____________ PLAN

17 BUSY ____________ ____________ BELT

18 PART ____________ ____________ CORD

19 COIN ____________ ____________ BARN

20 FLEX ____________ ____________ BREW

Total

Test 14: Mixed

Test time: 0 5 10 minutes

Rearrange the muddled words in capital letters in the following sentences so that they make sense.

Example There are sixty SNODCES _seconds_ in a UTMINE _minute_.

1 RAHSSK ________ are fierce predators that WDLEL ________ in the sea.

2 Half of VYSNTEE ________ is YRTHTI ________ five.

3 Myles prefers to play GBRYU ________ rather than BLFOOALT ________ .

4 There are many SHMLSEEO ________ people on the London TSERETS ________ .

5 The ISOTRHC ________ is the GELARTS ________ flightless bird.

Underline two words, one from each group, that go together to form a new word. The word in the first group always comes first.

Example (hand, green, for) (light, house, sure)

6 (kind, hard, for) (beds, nurses, wards)

7 (crack, break, mend) (slow, fast, full)

8 (grand, after, before) (day, noon, hour)

9 (pick, ball, match) (stick, nick, miss)

10 (water, free, tide) (sun, fall, wave)

Find and underline the two words that need to change places for each sentence to make sense.

Example She went to letter the write.

11 Please close the quietly door.

12 Marion more one mark got than Jason.

13 In the snow the dark was falling softly.

14 Her shirt birthday present was the favourite.

15 He likes to play Saturdays on football.

BROTH BROAD BROOM BROKE BROOK

If these words were written in alphabetical order which word would be:

16 first? ________

17 last? ________

Fill in the crossword so that all the words are included.

18–20 RARER SUGAR
SIDES SAFER
DRIER FLING

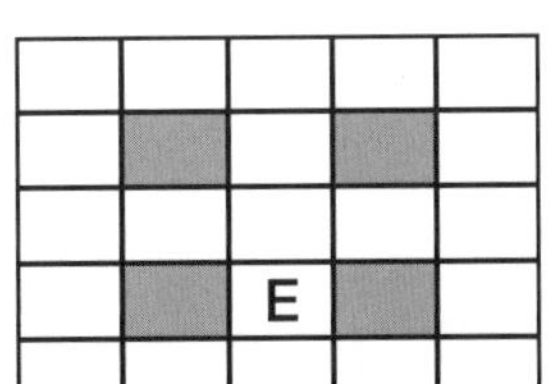

Total

Test 15: **Mixed**

Test time: 0 5 10 minutes

Complete the following sentences by selecting the most sensible word from each group of words given in the brackets. Underline the words selected.

Example The (children, boxes, foxes) carried the (houses, books, steps) home from the (greengrocer, library, factory).

1 The footballer (picked, kicked, licked) the (ice cream, apple, ball) into the (back, stomach, heart) of the net.

2 The business (deal, class, man) took his (newspaper, sandwiches, desk) out of his briefcase and began to (read, eat, write) it.

3 (Why, Who, How) can I help you with your homework if (he, she, you) haven't brought your (books, cushions, hats) home?

4 At midday the grandfather (clock, man, chair) in our hallway (chimes, jumps, talks) (two, eight, twelve) times.

5 In order to (sleep, climb, write) neatly you will need to (eat, sharpen, break) your (pencil, knife, rubber).

Underline the one word in each group that cannot be made from the letters of the word in capital letters.

Example	STATIONERY	stone	tyres	ration	nation	noisy
6	ELASTIC	stile	scale	steal	stick	slice
7	GRAPEFRUIT	pager	treat	tiger	grate	purge
8	SPLENDOUR	round	proud	unless	loner	drops
9	STRAIGHT	shirt	right	thirst	stride	tights
10	PLEASANT	least	stale	plane	nasal	please

The code for the word BRIGHTER is 56174236. Encode each of these words using the same code.

11 GRIT __________ **12** TRIBE __________

Decode these codes using the same code as above.

13 4365 __________ **14** 431742 __________ **15** 21736 __________

Give the two missing numbers in each sequence.

Example CQ DP EQ FP *GQ* *HP*

16 38 35 ___ 29 ___ 23

17 17 20 24 29 ___ ___

18 2 4 ___ 16 32 ___

19 5 16 6 18 ___ ___ 8 22

20 ___ 17 44 ___ 33 21 22 23

Total

Test time: 0 5 10 minutes

Fill in the crosswords so that all the words are included.

1–3

CHAIR RADAR
MOTOR CHASM
AWARD AWAIT

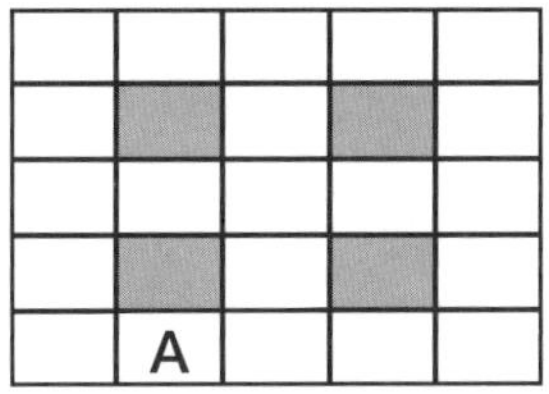

4–6

MEETS SHEDS
SOCKS OLIVE
CRIME STORM

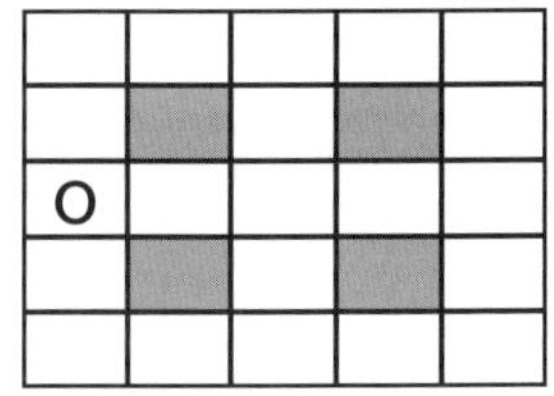

From the information supplied, underline the one statement below it that must be true.

7 My dustbin is black. My rubbish collection is on Thursdays.

A All black dustbins are emptied on Thursdays.
B My dustbin is emptied on Thursdays.
C Thursday is a convenient day for rubbish collection.
D My black dustbin is rubbish.

A B C D E F G H I J K L M N O P Q R S T U V W X Y Z

The word FLOWER is written in code as GMPXFS. Encode each of these words using the same code.

8 ROW ____________ **9** LEAF ____________

10 Decode TVOOZ using the same code. ____________

Move one letter from the first word to the second word to make two new words.

Example hunt sip hut snip

11 spear teak ____________ ____________
12 mange hue ____________ ____________
13 frail stay ____________ ____________
14 broom led ____________ ____________
15 tired tout ____________ ____________

Write the four-letter word hidden at the end of one word and the beginning of the next word. The order of the letters may not be changed.

Example We had bat<u>s and</u> balls. sand

16 It was remarkable how fast army tanks appeared. ____________
17 The Australians batted until eleven o'clock. ____________
18 Watch out, there is a hair on that piece of cake! ____________
19 I wish chocolate fountains would flow all the time. ____________
20 I catch the school bus to my village every day. ____________

Time for a break! Go to Puzzle Page 43

Total

Test 17: **Mixed**

Test time: 0 5 10 minutes

Look at these words. Sort them into groups.

1–4 Ford metre Berlin pineapple
Venice Vauxhall banana millimetre

A	B	C	D
Cars	Measurements	Cities	Fruit
___	___	___	___
___	___	___	___

Add one letter to the word in capital letters to make a new word. The meaning of the new word is given in the clue.

Example PLAN simple PLAIN

5 CEASE a fold in material ___

6 PLATE the roof of your mouth ___

7 READ not look forward to ___

8 TAPER to interfere with ___

Underline the two words that are the odd ones out in the following groups of words.

Example black king purple green house

9 ring circle necklace bracelet box

10 breakfast lunch cup plate dinner

11 finger nail tack screw shoe

12 bite tooth chew munch lip

Rearrange the letters in capitals to make another word. The new word has something to do with the first two words or phrases.

Example spot soil SAINT STAIN

13 brown breakfast bread STOAT ___

14 mouldy not fresh LEAST ___

15 surplus an extra one REAPS ___

16 wall covering covers a wound STAPLER ___

Complete the following sentences in the best way by choosing one word from each set of brackets.

Example Tall is to (tree, short, colour) as narrow is to (thin, white, wide).

17 King is to (crown, queen, kingdom) as judge is to (wig, jury, bench).

18 Fish is to (cod, scales, chips) as bird is to (beak, wing, feathers).

19 Deer is to (antlers, venison, fawn) as cow is to (steak, beef, milk).

20 Hammer is to (tool, nail, anvil) as spanner is to (screw, pin, nut).

Total

TEST 18: **Mixed**

Test time: 0 5 10 minutes

Underline one word in brackets that will go equally well with both the pairs of words outside the brackets.

Example	rush, attack	cost, fee	(price, hasten, strike, <u>charge</u>, money)
1	examine, inspect	stop, limit	(test, check, restrain, study)
2	correctly, properly	brim, rise	(right, well, simply, spring)
3	imitate, mirror	think, consider	(reflect, demonstrate, ponder, return)
4	boundary, edge	confine, curb	(margin, pavement, limit, restrict)
5	affordable, inexpensive	second-rate, inferior	(mean, reasonable, low, cheap)

A B C D E F G H I J K L M N O P Q R S T U V W X Y Z

Fill in the missing letters. The alphabet has been written out to help you.

Example AB is to CD as PQ is to <u>RS</u>.

6 ACF is to GIL as MOR is to ________.

7 ZX is to WU as TR is to ________.

8 ZA is to XC as VE is to ________.

9 ZW is to TQ as NK is to ________.

10 AmD is to GnJ as MoP is to ________.

In her basket, Amy had beans, carrots, cucumber, mushrooms and tomatoes. Work out which section of the supermarket shelves she found her items on.

11–15

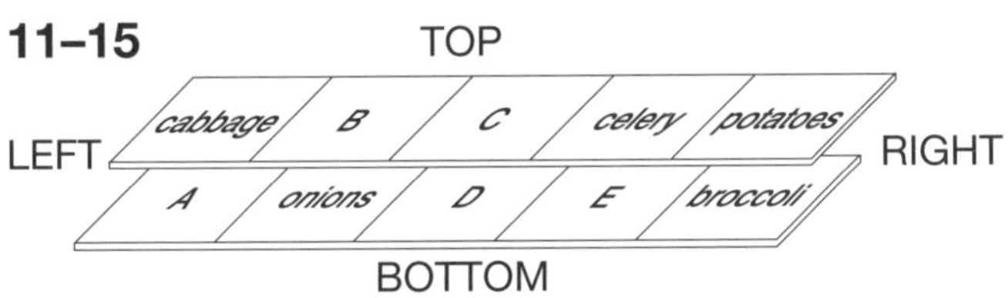

The beans were somewhere above the mushrooms.
The cucumber was somewhere to the left of the tomatoes but not under the carrots.
The carrots, in turn, were directly above the mushrooms.

A = ____________________

B = ____________________

C = ____________________

D = ____________________

E = ____________________

Look at the first group of three words. The word in the middle has been made from the two other words. Complete the second group of three words in the same way, making a new word in the middle of the group.

Example	PA<u>IN</u>	INTO	<u>TO</u>OK	ALSO	<u>SOON</u>	ONLY
16	SLAP	LACK	DOCK	PICK	________	HEED
17	SORT	STOP	OPEN	FEEL	________	OXEN
18	POOL	LOVE	SAVE	SEAL	________	LIMB
19	MASH	SALE	TEAL	WAGE	________	PERT
20	FLAG	GLAD	DRAB	SLIP	________	GRUB

Total

TEST 19: **Mixed**

Test time: 0 5 10 minutes

Underline the two words, one from each group, which are the most opposite in meaning.

Example (dawn, early, wake) (late, stop, sunrise)

1	(off, under, up)	(on, through, by)
2	(steaming, warm, icy)	(cool, sleet, cold)
3	(for, again, by)	(up, through, against)
4	(leave, grant, give)	(pull, apply, take)
5	(point, sharp, apex)	(notice, blunt, hill)

A B C D E F G H I J K L M N O P Q R S T U V W X Y Z

Give the two missing groups of letters in the following sequences. The alphabet has been written out to help you.

Example CQ DP EQ FP GQ HP

6	AC	EG	IK	MO	QS	____	____
7	ZP	YQ	XR	WS	VT	____	____
8	CAD	DBE	ECF	FDG	GEH	____	____
9	AZ	CX	EV	GT	IR	____	____
10	feg	gfh	hgi	ihj	jik	____	____

Find the letter which will end the first word and start the second word.

Example peac (h) ome

11 clea (__) eign

12 spac (__) njoy

13 tric (__) icks

14 rel (__) ell

15 tune (__) esk

Here are the number codes for four words.
9413 9471 7413 9331
Match the right code to each word.

16 LACK ________

17 LAKE ________

18 LEEK ________

19 CAKE ________

Decode this word using the same code as above.

20 1493 ________

Total

Test 20: **Mixed**

Test time: 0 5 10 minutes

Write the four-letter word hidden at the end of one word and the beginning of the next word. The order of the letters may not be changed.

Example We had bat<u>s and</u> balls. sand

1 We saw nothing but desert stretching before us. ______
2 Mrs Smith knelt down to dust under the table. ______
3 Neither the zebra nor the antelope heard the lion. ______
4 The pies are in the oven. ______
5 Some people think taking vitamins helps stop illnesses spreading. ______

From the information supplied, underline the one statement below it that must be true.

6 French is taught at our school. Our class has a French lesson on Friday.

A All schools teach French.
B We have a French lesson on Friday.
C French is taught only on Friday.
D Our school is in France.

The code for the word CLOTHES is written as @!+?/*£. Decode these words using the same code as above.

7 @+£? ______ 8 £@/++! ______ 9 @/**£* ______

Encode these words using the same code as above.

10 HOTEL ______ 11 THOSE ______

Complete the following sentences in the best way by choosing one word from each set of brackets.

Example Tall is to (tree, <u>short</u>, colour) as narrow is to (thin, white, <u>wide</u>).

12 Pen is to (paper, write, biro) as brush is to (paint, blue, easel).
13 Water is to bottle as (milk, petrol, meat) is to (mouth, garage, carton).
14 (Trousers, Top, Under) is to bottom as high is to (above, over, low).
15 Mind is to (think, read, care) as stomach is to (digest, fat, ache).
16 Go is to (get, come, stop) as green is to (amber, red, light).

If a = 5, b = 4, c = 3, d = 2 and e = 1, find the value of the following.

17 $(a + b) - (c + d) =$ ______
18 $\frac{bc}{d} =$ ______
19 $(d^2 + c^2) - e =$ ______
20 $\frac{be}{d} + a =$ ______

Total

TEST 21: **Mixed**

Test time: 0 5 10 minutes

Find a word that is similar in meaning to the word in capital letters and that rhymes with the second word.

Example CABLE tyre wire

1 ENCLOSURE dense ______ 2 LIQUID course ______

3 CONFUSE cuddle ______ 4 SHARE mice ______

Find a word that can be put in front of each of the following words to make a new, compound word.

Example cast fall word pour down

5 fall mark proof colour ______

6 fighter work side arm ______

7 man drop ball flake ______

8 forest drop coat bow ______

If these words are placed in alphabetical order, which comes fourth?

9 flatworm flatbed fledgling flannel flank ______

10 stagnant stagecoach stagger stadium stainless ______

11 harness harmonic harelip harpoon harrier ______

12 larder larva larceny lapwing largesse ______

Find the three-letter word that can be added to the letters in capitals to make a new word. The new word will complete the sentence sensibly. Write the three-letter word.

Example The cat sprang onto the MO. USE

13 Our car has new tyres on each WH. ______

14 The headmaster said my H was too long and needed cutting. ______

15 There are not enough chairs so he is STING. ______

16 CRIES are a red fruit with a stone in the middle. ______

A B C D E F G H I J K L M N O P Q R S T U V W X Y Z

Give the two missing pairs of letters in the following sequences. The alphabet has been written out to help you.

Example CQ DP EQ FP GQ HP

17 AX DU GR JO ML ___ ___ 18 WV YX AZ CB ED ___ ___

19 GQ HQ IR JR KS ___ ___ 20 BW BV CU CT DS ___ ___

Total

Test 22: **Mixed**

Test time: 0 5 10 minutes

Underline the pair of words most opposite in meaning.

Example cup, mug coffee, milk <u>hot, cold</u>

1	win, lose	win, success	failure, disappointment
2	hot, cool	warm, cool	cold, warm
3	clear, lucid	cloudy, rainy	clear, cloudy
4	stand, deliver	collect, deliver	send, deliver

Find the missing number by using the two numbers outside the brackets in the same way as the other sets of numbers.

Example 2 [8] 4 3 [18] 6 5 [25] 5

5	7 [10] 1	3 [18] 5	4 [___] 2
6	14 [11] 4	13 [7] 7	12 [___] 3
7	5 [15] 2	7 [5] 6	4 [___] 3
8	6 [8] 7	7 [6] 4	8 [___] 3

Underline the word the brackets which goes best with the words given outside the brackets.

Example word, paragraph, sentence (pen, cap, <u>letter</u>, top, stop)

9	rush, dash, shoot	(arrow, dart, rifle, move, jog)
10	honest, light, just	(true, pale, dark, fair, time)
11	remove, expel, emit	(take, school, bully, reject, eject)
12	rotund, portly, heavy	(weight, harbour, stout, stone, round)

Move one letter from the first word to the second word to make two new words.

Example hunt sip <u>hut</u> <u>snip</u>

13	crane	bed	________	________
14	plight	car	________	________
15	suet	urn	________	________
16	flood	hit	________	________

Underline the two words that are made from the same letters.

Example TAP PET <u>TEA</u> POT <u>EAT</u>

17	SHEARS	SHEEP	SHAPES	PHASES	SHORTS
18	STRONG	GRUNTS	GRANTS	STRAIN	STRUNG
19	STAPLE	PLEASE	PALEST	APPLES	SCRAPE
20	BLAST	STOLE	STALE	LABEL	LEAST

Total

Test 23: Mixed

Test time: 0 5 10 minutes

Look at these groups of words.

A	B	C	D	E
pencil	oak	seaside	table	trout
ruler	elm	sandcastle	cupboard	carp

Choose the correct group for each of these words below. Write in the group letter.

1–5 beech _____ rubber _____ perch _____ pike _____ beach _____

bed _____ pen _____ pine _____ chair _____ seaweed _____

Remove one letter from the word in capital letters to leave a new word. The meaning of the new word is given in the clue.

Example AUNT an insect ANT

6 FRAME well known __________

7 CHEAT to make hotter __________

8 PLANT organise __________

9 CRATER supply __________

10 LADDER snake __________

Underline the word in the brackets that is most opposite in meaning to the word in capitals.

Example WIDE (broad, vague, long, narrow, motorway)

11 THIN (thick, healthy, full, emaciated, skinny)

12 EASY (simple, facile, difficult, descriptive, quick)

13 FULL (avoid, replete, refill, empty, complete)

14 FLAT (level, uneven, square, apartment, deflated)

15 QUIET (noisy, quite, crowded, whispering, tranquil)

Underline the pair of words most similar in meaning.

Example come, go roams, wanders fear, fare

16 high, low climb, ascend lift, descend

17 polite, impolite before, now concur, agree

18 healthy, well well, lake health, happiness

19 dart, dodge dodge, budge arrow, dart

20 pillow, bed carpet, rug bucket, spade

Total

TEST 1: Similars and Opposites (page 2)

1 **tidy, scruffy** 'Tidy' means neat whereas 'scruffy' means untidy.
2 **broad, narrow** 'Broad' means wide whereas 'narrow' means thin.
3 **unwell, healthy** 'Unwell' means ill whereas 'healthy' means well.
4 **pale, flushed** A 'pale' face looks very white whereas a 'flushed' face is reddened.
5 **protect** 6 **piece**
7 **tie** 8 **tiny**
9 **few, many** 10 **stupid, sensible**
11 **present, absent** 12 **far, near**
13 **silence** The closest in meaning to 'QUIET' is 'silence' because they both mean the absence of noise.
14 **group** The closest in meaning to 'CLASS' is 'group' as both mean a collection or gathering of people.
15 **shred** The closest in meaning to 'TEAR' is 'shred' as they both mean to rip up into pieces.
16 **question** The closest in meaning to 'QUERY' is 'question' as they both mean to ask, request or enquire.
17 **laugh** To 'cry' can be a result of being 'upset'. The result of 'happy' can be to 'laugh'.
18 **against** 'Left' and 'right' are antonyms in the same way 'for' and 'against' are the opposite of each other.
19 **ankle** A 'finger' is part of a hand attached to a 'wrist'. A 'toe' is part of a foot attached to an 'ankle'.
20 **keep** 'Reveal' and 'show' are synonyms, as are 'retain' and 'keep'.

TEST 2: Sorting Words (page 3)

1 **claw** A 'claw' can be like a nail or hook and, as a verb, mean to scrape or graze.
2 **level** 'Level' can mean smooth and also a rank or height of something.
3 **tip** 'Tip' means to let fall; it also means the top of something like the apex of a mountain.
4 **place** 'Place' is the whereabouts of something or how you use or employ something.
5 **pure** 'Pure' is fresh and unsullied and, particularly if applied to a person, means natural and genuine.
6 **basket, kitchen** 7 **outside, jacket**
8 **English, lesson** 9 **library, varied**
10 **school, camping** 11 **THORN**
12 **CLASP** 13 **BLEAT**
14 **THROB** 15 **DENIM**
16 The **toilet** sign has fallen off the **door**.
17 You have arrived **just** in **time** for tea.
18 Why have you put your **shoes** on the wrong **feet**?
19 In a **storm**, the **park** bench was blown over.
20 The **leaves** fall during **autumn**.

TEST 3: Selecting Words (page 4)

1 **r** rage, rally, rat, roar, reach
2 **v** vice, van, valley, vomit, vow
3 **c** chunk, clash, chip, crush, craft
4 **m** mash, malign, mutter, meat, mail
5 **id** squid, idea
6 **re** spare, really
7 **st** twist, stop
8 **th** both, thorn
9 **troublesome**
10 **invest** 11 **begun** 12 **endless**
13 **lane** A 'lane' is a thoroughfare in the same way as a 'road', a 'street' and an 'avenue'.
14 **foot** 'Toes', 'ankle' and 'heel' are all parts of the 'foot'.
15 **pen** All the words are items of stationery.
16 **trainer** All the words are items of footwear or shoes.
17 **crate** 18 **stone**
19 **slope** 20 **folder**

TEST 4: Finding Words (page 5)

1 **leap** A long icic**le ap**peared on her windowsill last night.
2 **howl** he ghostly sound of bot**h owls** could be heard
3 **vest** My cousins ha**ve st**ones all around their pond.
4 **cell** In an airport lounge any unattended par**cel l**ooks suspicious.
5 **mint** Pour the crea**m int**o the striped jug please.
6 **ATE** water
7 **ILL** village
8 **SIN** crossing
9 **YES** eyes
10 **PEA** speaking
11 **super** supermarket, supermodel, supernatural, superstar
12 **some** something, somehow, somewhat, somebody
13 **eye** eyewitness, eyeshadow, eyebrow, eyeball
14 **rain** raindrop, raincoat, rainforest, rainbow
15 **life** lifeguard, lifeboat, lifestyle, lifetime
16 **a** bred, taint
17 **g** bun, gamble
18 **t** wan, pint
19 **l** bride, growling
20 **h** wine, hearth

TEST 5: Alphabetical Order and Substitution (page 6)

1–5 Use grids to help you.

1 **circle**

c	a	l	l	e	d		1st
c	h	a	r	g	e		2nd
c	i	r	c	l	e		3rd
c	o	l	o	u	r		4th
c	u	r	r	i	e	s	5th

2 **quaver**

q	u	a	r	r	y		1st
q	u	a	r	t	z		2nd
q	u	a	v	e	r		3rd
q	u	e	e	n			4th
q	u	i	l	t	s		5th

3 **drench**

d	r	a	g	o	n		1st
d	r	e	a	m	s		2nd
d	r	e	n	c	h		3rd
d	r	i	n	k	s		4th
d	r	o	w	s	y		5th

4 **pillow**

p	a	l	a	c	e		1st
p	a	n	d	a	s		2nd
p	i	l	l	o	w		3rd
p	l	a	c	e	d		4th
p	l	a	n	e	t		5th

5 **galaxy**

g	a	b	l	e	s		1st
g	a	i	n	e	d		2nd
g	a	l	a	x	y		3rd
g	a	l	l	o	p		4th
g	a	r	d	e	n		5th

6 **7** $(10 + 3) - 6 = 7$
7 **60** $10 \times 6 = 60$
8 **36** $(24 \div 4) \times 6 = 36$
9 **16** $(24 - 10) + (6 - 4) = 16$
10 **p** $(24 - 4) - 10 = 10$ $10 = p$
11 **u** $4 \times 3 \times 2 = 24$ $24 = u$
12 **u** $(10 \times 3) - 6 = 24$ $24 = u$
13 **s** $(4 \times 4) - 10 = 6$ $6 = s$
14 **r** $(4 \times 6) \div 24 + 2 = 3$ $3 = r$
15 **r** $(6 + 24) \div 10 = 3$ $3 = r$
16 **17** $4 + 3 + 2 + 1 + 5 + 2 = 17$
17 **16** $4 + 3 + 2 + 1 + 6 = 16$
18 **17** $3 + 2 + 1 + 5 + 6 = 17$
19 **21** $5 + 6 + 1 + 4 + 3 + 2 = 21$
20 **5** Take the letters 'PALE' out of 'LAPSE', it leaves 'S' which equals 5.

TEST 6: Word Progressions (page 7)

1–4 Use grids as shown below to help work out the missing word.

1 **PLAN**

1	2	3*	
G	R	I	N

4	3*		
P	I	N	K

1	2	3*	
P	L	U	G

4	3*		
N	A	V	E

2 **ELSE**

	2	1	
T	I	M	E

3			4
L	O	O	K

	2	1	
S	L	E	D

3			4
S	O	R	E

3 **TRAY**

2		1	4*
P	A	S	T

4*	3		
T	O	R	N

2		1	4*
R	O	T	A

4*	3		
Y	A	W	N

4 **NAVE**

	2		1/4*
D	U	M	B

3		1/4*	
L	O	B	E

	2		1/4*
L	A	W	N

3		1/4*	
V	E	E	R

5 **LOOM, LOOK**
6 **CUBE, CURE**
7 **BOAT, BEAT**
8 **FORT, FORM**
9 **DIRT, DART**
10 **TAME, SAME**
11 **sole** The 'age' of the first word in each pair changes to 'ole' in the second word.
12 **bout** The 'ea' of the first word in each pair changes to 'ou' in the second word.
13 **isle** The first and last letters of the first words are removed in the second word.
14 **toll** The first and third letters of the first word are removed in the second word.
15–20 Solve these questions by looking at the first set of three and working out how the first and last numbers have been used to arrive at the middle number. Apply this to the second set of three and see if it works. If it does, apply it to the last set.
15 **45** $7 \times 4 = 28$ and $6 \times 3 = 18$, so $9 \times 5 = 45$
16 **24** $(4 + 1) \times 2 = 10$ and $(3 + 6) \times 2 = 18$, so $(5 + 7) \times 2 = 24$

17 **3** 7 ÷ 7 = 1 and 6 ÷ 3 = 2, so 12 ÷ 4 = 3
18 **2** (5 × 4) – 10 = 10 and (3 × 8) – 10 = 14, so (2 × 6) – 10 = 2
19 **17** 4 + 3 = 7 and 9 + 8 = 17, so 11 + 6 = 17
20 **1** (6 × 2) – 2 = 10 and (5 × 3) – 3 = 12, so (2 × 1) – 1 = 1

TEST 7: Logic (page 8)

1–6 From the information you know that History is opposite Geography, so they must be in both Room 3 and Room 8 as no other rooms are directly opposite each other. In the last sentence you learn that Maths is next door to both Geography and Science. Only three rooms are directly next door to each other. So, Science 5, Maths 4, Geography 3 and therefore, History 8. This leaves English and French. The first sentence states that English has a lower number than French, so English 1 and French 7.

1 **Room 1: English**
2 **Room 3: Geography**
3 **Room 4: Maths**
4 **Room 5: Science**
5 **Room 7: French**
6 **Room 8: History**

7–11 Use the compass points and the map to help you.

CAMP	MOUNTAINS	
JUNGLE	SWAMP	
		EXPLORER

7 **jungle** 8 **mountains** 9 **north**
10 **west** 11 **north-west**

12–20 A table is the easiest way to sort the information, like this:

	Rabbits	Goldfish	Cat	Dog	Gerbil	Tortoise
Darren	✓			✓		
William	✓			✓	✓	
Sita	✓	✓	✓			✓
Jane	✓	✓	✓			
Phil	✓					✓
Brett		✓	✓		✓	
Sven		✓	×			
Sandy					✓	

12 **6** 13–14 **rabbit and dog**
15 **8** 16–17 **Sandy and Sven**
18 **William** 19 **Brett** 20 **Sita**

TEST 8: Simple Codes (page 9)

1 **1946** T = 1, R = 9, U = 4, E = 6
2 **9438** R = 9, U = 4, M = 3, P = 8
3 **MORE** 3 = M, 2 = O, 9 = R, 6 = E
4 **PORT** 8 = P, 2 = O, 9 = R, 1 = T
5 **NEST** A = N, J = E, O = S, Z = T
6 **STEP** O = S, Z = T, J = E, R = P
7 **£ + x –** M = £, A = +, L = x, E = –
8 **@ + $ –** R = @, A = +, C = $, E = –

9–13 Two words begin with 'T' so T = 4. Two words end 'ST' so S = 3 and T = 4. Knowing these number and letter pairings will allow you to work out the rest.

9 **TAME** 4 = T, 6 = A, 1 = M, 7 = E
10 **TEST** 4 = T, 7 = E, 3 = S, 4 = T
11 **STEM** 3 = S, 4 = T, 7 = E, 1 = M
12 **MAST** 1 = M, 6 = A, 3 = S, 4 = T
13 **EAST** 7 = E, 6 = A, 3 = S, 4 = T
14 **MEAT** 1 = M, 7 = E, 6 = A, 4 = T

15–20 Two of the codes end 'm 9', so m = T and 9 = S. The code beginning '9 m' therefore is 'STAR'. Knowing these number and letter pairings will allow you to work out the rest.

15 **m X % 3** T = m, U = X, R = %, N = 3
16 **% Q m 9** R = %, A = Q, T = m, S = 9
17 **9 m Q %** S = 9, T = m, A = Q, R = %
18 **3 X m 9** N = 3, U = X, T = m, S = 9
19 **9 m X 3 m** S = 9, T = m, U = X, N = 3, T = m
20 **9 Q m X % 3** S = 9, A = Q, T = m, U = X, R = %, N = 3

TEST 9: More Complicated Codes (page 10)

1 **TPDDFS** To get from the word to the code, move each letter forwards one place.
2 **GOAL** To get from the code to the word, move each letter backwards one place.
3–4 To get from the word to the code, move each letter forwards two places.
3 **LCO** 4 **BGDTC**
5–6 To get from the word to the code, move each letter backwards three places.
5 **QXYIB** 6 **MFKH**
7–8 To get from the code to the word, move each letter forwards three places.
7 **PART** 8 **JADE**
9–13 Use a grid to help you.

A	B	C	D	E	F	G	H	I	J
1	2	3	4	5	6	7	8	9	10

9 **6554** 10 **3175** 11 **8514**
12 **FACE** 13 **HEDGE**
14 **QJKY** To get from the word to the code, move each letter forwards five places.
15–20 Use a grid to help you.

B	L	A	C	K
e	o	d	f	n

You know d = A and n = K. Two of the codes end 'dun'. Therefore, looking at the words, you can work out that u must be the code for R. So BARK = edun and LARK = odun. Two of the words begin with P so s = P. You can complete all the words and codes except the final letters represented by 'b' and 'q'. Therefore, go back to BLACK and the original code in the grid. Note the relationship between the letters and the code. To get from the word to the code, you move each letter forwards. To get from the code to the word, move backwards 3 places, so b = Y and q = N.

15 **edun** B = e, A = d, R = u, K = n
16 **sodb** P = s, L = o, A = d, Y = b
17 **odun** L = o, A = d, R = u, K = n
18 **sodq** P = s, L = o, A = d, N = q
19 **BIRD** e = B, l = I, u = R, g = D
20 **FLEW** i = F, o = L, h = E, z = W

TEST 10: Sequences (page 11)

1 **bird, insect** An 'ostrich' is a bird as a 'fly' is an 'insect'.
2 **talk, stride** To 'speak' means to converse or 'talk' as to 'pace' means to step or 'stride'.
3 **funny, sad** 'Hilarious' means extremely amusing or 'funny' as 'tragic' means extremely 'sad'.
4 **GFE** All three letters move backwards three places.
5 **LJ** Both letters move forwards two places.
6 **Jq** Both letters move forwards three places.
7 **T8** The letters move backwards two places. The numbers decrease by 1.
8 **S18t** Both letters move forward two places, and the second letter also changes from capitals (upper case) to lower case. The numbers in between them increase by 2.
9 **dW** The lower case letters are in alphabetical order. The capital letters are in reverse alphabetical order.
10 **GL** Both letters move forwards two places.
11 **30, 8** This is an alternating pattern. The first, third and fifth numbers increase by 10. The second, fourth and sixth numbers increase by 2.
12 **lj, Kl** This is a consecutive pattern of the next alphabetical place. The first letter is in capitals, the second in lower case.
13 **11, xx** This is an alternating pattern. The numbers decrease by 11. The letters are in pairs and move backwards one place.
14 **27y, 30b** The numbers increase by 3. The letters move forward by three places. When you come to the end of the alphabet, wrap round to the beginning again: xyzabcC.
15 **2, 4** The numbers increase by doubling each time.
16 **4, 18** This is an alternating pattern. The first, third, fifth and seventh numbers increase by 6. The second, fourth, sixth and eighth numbers increase by 4.
17 **2, 4** This is an alternating pattern. The first, third, fifth and seventh numbers increase by 2. The second, fourth, sixth and eighth number is doubled each time.
18 **c7X, d9W** The lower case letter moves forward by one place. The number increases by 2. The capital letters move backwards one place.
19 **12, 12** This is an alternating pattern. The first, third, fifth and seventh numbers increase by 4. The second, fourth, sixth and eighth numbers increase by 3.
20 **4Y, 9W** The number added increases by 1 each time: +1, +2, +3, +4, +5, +6, +7. The letters are in reverse alphabetical order.

TEST 11: Mixed (page 12)

1–5 Category A is games (**hockey, football**).
Category B is metals (**steel, platinum**).
Category C is birds (**flamingo, seagull**).
Category D is colours (**purple, azure**).
Category E is weather types (**hail, sun**).
6 **sp** clasp, spoon
7 **el** swivel, elect
8 **le** style, lemon
9 **sh** varnish, shout
10 **ic** panic, icicle
11 **TALE** 12 **LIMB** 13 **BRIDE**
14 **OWL** 15 **STEP**
16 **door, car** The other words are all types of footwear.
17 **beetroot, carrot** The other words are all fruit.
18 **salmon, crocodile** The other words are all mammals.
19 **camera, binoculars** The other words you listen to.
20 **lake, pond** The other words all contain trees.

TEST 12: Mixed (page 13)

1 **disappear, vanish** Both the words mean to go from view, to become invisible.
2 **competent, capable** Both words mean experienced, skilled.

3 **scarlet, crimson** Both words are shades of red.
4 **scamper, scurry** Both words mean to dash or hurry.
5 **wasteful, uneconomical** Both words means extravagant, careless, inefficient.
6 **stop** Please remember you must open each window slowly.
7 **whom** I avoided the girl who made me cry.
8 **hero** The rope bridge swung in the breeze.
9 **keep** Explorers make epic journeys across the globe.
10 **scar** Tom's ball dented the wing of his father's car.
11 **A** You must use only the information given. B, C and D may or may not be true. They are not mentioned therefore you must reject them.
12 **d** build, drown
13 **p** stamp, proud
14 **e** twice, endure
15 **y** daisy, yearn
16 **10** 2 + 5 + 3 = 10
17 **8** 1 + 5 + 2 = 8
18 **14** 4 + 3 + 5 + 2 = 14
19 **10** 2 + 1 + 4 + 3 = 10
20 **15** 4 + 3 + 5 + 2 + 1 = 15

TEST 13: Mixed (page 14)

1–5 Two of the codes have '22' in the middle. Therefore 2 = O. Two of the codes begin with '3'. Therefore, 3 = F. Knowing these letter and number pairings will allow you to work out the rest.
1 **3526** F = 3, R = 5, O = 2, M = 6
2 **5223** R = 5, O = 2, F = 3
3 **3256** F = 3, O = 2, R = 5, M = 6
4 **6225** M = 6, O = 2, R = 5
5 **ROOM** R = 5, O = 2, M = 6
6 **spin** I was stung by a wasp in my garden.
7 **then** In the dusk the nightingales were singing.
8 **inch** The team stays in cheap hotels to save money.
9 **drop** The tide tugged at the tarred rope holding the anchor.
10 **reel** Ben and his friends consumed three loaves of bread.
11 **share**
12 **chat**
13 **toil**
14 **climb**
15 **earth**
16 **FLAT, FLAN**
17 **BUST, BEST**
18 **CART, CARD**
19 **CORN, BORN**
20 **FLEW, BLEW**

TEST 14: Mixed (page 15)

1 **SHARKS, DWELL**
2 **SEVENTY, THIRTY**
3 **RUGBY, FOOTBALL**
4 **HOMELESS, STREETS**
5 **OSTRICH, LARGEST**
6 **forwards**
7 **breakfast**
8 **afternoon**
9 **matchstick**
10 **waterfall**
11 Please close the door quietly.
12 Marion got one mark more than Jason.
13 In the dark the snow was falling softly.
14 Her favourite birthday present was the shirt.
15 He likes to play football on Saturdays.
16–17 Arrange the words in a grid to make it easier to put them in the correct alphabetical order.

B	R	O	A	D		1ST
B	R	O	K	E		2ND
B	R	O	O	M		3RD
B	R	O	T	H		4TH

16 **BROAD**
17 **BROTH**

18–20

S	I	D	E	S
A	■	R	■	U
F	L	I	N	G
E	■	E	■	A
R	A	R	E	R

TEST 15: Mixed (page 16)

1–5 Try each of the words in the first set of brackets. Do they make sense with any words in the second and third set of brackets? Only one combination of three words makes sense.
1 **kicked, ball, back**
2 **man, newspaper, read**
3 **How, you, books**
4 **clock, chimes, twelve**
5 **write, sharpen, pencil**
6 **stick** There is no 'k' in ELASTIC'.
7 **treat** There is only one 'T' in GRAPEFRUIT.
8 **unless** There is only one 'S' in SPLENDOUR'.
9 **stride** There is no 'E' and no 'D' in 'STRAIGHT'.
10 **please** There is only one 'E' in 'PLEASANT'.
11–15 Use a grid to help you.

B	R	I	G	H	T	E	R
5	6	1	7	4	2	3	6

11 **7612** G = 7, R = 6, I = 1, T = 2
12 **26153** T = 2, R = 6, I = 1, B = 5, E = 3
13 **HERB** 4 = H, 3 = E, 6 = R, 5 = B
14 **HEIGHT** 4 = H, 3 = E, 1 = I, 7 = G, 4 = H, 2 = T
15 **TIGER** 2 = T, 1 = I, 7 = G, 3 = E, 6 = R
16 **32, 26** Each number decreases by 3.
17 **35, 42** The number added increases by one each time: +3, +4, +5 +6 +7.
18 **8, 64** The number doubles each time, so 4 × 2 = 8 and 32 × 2 = 64.

19 **7, 20** This is an alternating pattern. The first, third, fifth and seventh numbers increase by 1. The second, fourth, sixth and eighth numbers increase by 2.

20 **55, 19** This is an alternating pattern. The first, third, fifth and seventh numbers decrease by 11. The second, fourth, sixth and eighth numbers increase by 2.

TEST 16: Mixed (page 17)

1–3

C	H	A	S	M
H	■	W	■	O
A	W	A	I	T
I	■	R	■	O
R	A	D	A	R

4–6

S	O	C	K	S
T	■	R	■	H
O	L	I	V	E
R	■	M	■	D
M	E	E	T	S

7 **B** A, C and D may or may not be true. You must use only the information that is given.

8–10 To get from the word to the code, move the letters forwards one place.

8 **SPX** R = S, O = P, W = X

9 **MFBG** L = M, E = F, A = B, F = G

10 **SUNNY** To get from the code to the word, move the letters backwards one place. T = S, V = U, O = N, Z = Y

11 **s** pear, steak

12 **g** mane, huge

13 **r** fail, stray

14 **b** room, bled

15 **r** tied, trout

16 **star** It was remarkable how fast army tanks appeared.

17 **tile** The Australians batted until eleven o'clock.

18 **iron** Watch out, there is a hair on that piece of cake.

19 **wall** I wish chocolate fountains would flow all the time.

20 **bust** I catch the school bus to my village every day.

TEST 17: Mixed (page 18)

1–4 **A Ford, Vauxhall**
B metre, millimetre
C Berlin, Venice
D pineapple, banana

5 **CREASE** 6 **PALATE**

7 **DREAD** 8 **TAMPER**

9 **circle, box** The other words are items of jewellery.

10 **cup, plate** The other words are meals.

11 **finger, shoe** The other words are metal fixings.

12 **tooth, lip** The other words mean to gnaw or chomp.

13 **TOAST** 14 **STALE**

15 **SPARE** 16 **PLASTER**

17 **crown, wig** A 'king' wears a 'crown' as a 'judge' wears a 'wig'.

18 **scales, feathers** A 'fish' has 'scales' on its body in the same way a 'bird' has 'feathers'.

19 **venison, beef** 'venison' is 'deer' meat as 'beef' is 'cow' meat.

20 **nail, nut** A 'hammer' hits a 'nail' in place as a 'spanner' turns a 'nut'.

TEST 18: Mixed (page 19)

1 **check** 'Check' means to look at something carefully and also to restrain oneself.

2 **well** 'Well' means something done right and also to come to the brim, like tears in your eyes.

3 **reflect** To 'reflect' something is to show the image back again and also to ponder about a matter.

4 **limit** A 'limit' is the margin or perimeter; it also means to check or restrict something.

5 **cheap** A 'cheap' price is a low or reasonable one and 'cheap' can also mean low-grade or shoddy.

6 **SUX** Each letter moves forward six places.

7 **QO** Each letter moves backwards three places.

8 **TG** The first letter moves backwards two places. The second letter moves forward two places.

9 **HE** Each letter moves backwards six places.

10 **SpV** The capital letters (first and third letters) move forward six places. The lower case letter, in the middle, moves forward one place.

11–15 The final sentence in the information says the carrots are directly above the mushrooms. Therefore, the carrots must be C and the mushrooms D. The first sentence tells us the beans are on the top shelf, therefore B. If the cucumber is left of the tomatoes, they must be A, leaving the tomatoes in E.

A = **cucumber**
B = **beans**
C = **carrots**
D = **mushrooms**
E = **tomatoes**

16–20 Use grids as shown below to help work out the missing word.

16 **ICED**

	1	2	
S	L	A	P

		3	4
D	O	C	K

	1	2	
P	I	C	K

		3	4
H	E	E	D

17 **FLEX**

1	3*		2
S	O	R	T

3*	4		
O	P	E	N

1	3*		2
F	E	E	L

3*	4		
O	X	E	N

18 **LAMB**

	2*	2*	1
P	O	O	L

		3	4
S	A	V	E

	2*	2*	1
S	E	A	L

		3	4
L	I	M	B

19 **GATE**

	2*	1	
M	A	S	H

	4	2*	3
T	E	A	L

	2*	1	
W	A	G	E

	4	2*	3
P	E	R	T

20 **PLUG**

	2	3*	1
F	L	A	G

4		3*	
D	R	A	B

	2	3*	1
S	L	I	P

4		3*	
G	R	U	B

TEST 19: Mixed (page 20)

1 **off, on** Out of all the prepositions, these are the most opposite.

2 **warm, cool** 'Warm' is on the way to being hot in the way 'cool' is to cold, therefore they are the most opposite.

3 **for, against** 'For' is pro something and 'against' is anti or contrary to it.

4 **give, take** 'Give' is going away from you and 'take' is coming towards you.

5 **sharp, blunt** A 'sharp' pencil has a pointed end whereas a 'blunt' one is rounded and smooth.

6 **UW, YA** In each pair, the letters are moving forwards four places.

7 **UU, TV** The first letters are in reverse alphabetical order. The second letters are in alphabetical order.

8 **HFI, IGJ** Each of the letters is in alphabetical order and moves forwards one place each time.

9 **KP, MN** The first letters move forwards two places. The second letters move backwards two letters.

10 **kjl, lkm** Each of the letters is in alphabetical order and moves forwards one place each time.

11 **r** clear, reign

12 **e** space, enjoy

13 **k** trick, kicks

14 **y** rely, yell

15 **d** tuned, desk

16–20 Three of the codes start with 9, so 9 = L. 3 = E as it is the only repeating number for the double E in LEEK. Knowing these number and letter pairings will allow you to work out the rest.

16 **9471** L = 9, A = 4, C = 7, K = 1

17 **9413** L = 9, A = 4, K = 1, E = 3

18 **9331** L = 9, E = 3, K = 1

19 **7413** C = 7, A = 4, K = 1, E = 3

20 **KALE** 1 = K, 4 = A, 9 = L, 3 = E

TEST 20: Mixed (page 21)

1 **sawn** We **saw n**othing but desert stretching before us.

2 **stun** Mrs Smith knelt down to du**st un**der the table.

3 **bran** Neither the ze**bra n**or the antelope heard the lion.

4 **rein** The pies a**re in** the oven.

5 **pill** Some people think taking vitamins helps sto**p ill**nesses spreading.

6 **B** A, C and D may or may not be correct. However, they should be rejected as they are not referred to in the given information.

7–11 Use a grid to help you.

C	L	O	T	H	E	S
@	!	+	?	/	*	£

7 **COST** @ = C, + = O, £ = S, ? = T

8 **SCHOOL** £ = S, @ = C, / = H, + = O, + = O, ! = L

9 **CHEESE** @ = C, / = H, *= E, * = E, £ = S, * = E

10 **/ + ? * !** H = /, O = +, T = ?, E = *, L = !

11 **? / + £ *** T = ?, H = /, O = +, S = £, E = *

12 **write, paint** You 'write' with a 'pen' in the same way you 'paint' with a 'brush'.

13 **milk, carton** 'Water' often comes in a 'bottle' in the same way as 'milk' comes in a 'carton'.

14 **Top, low** 'Top' is an antonym of 'bottom' in the same way as 'high' is to 'low'.

15 **think, digest** A 'mind' 'thinks' in a similar way to a 'stomach' 'digests'.

16 **stop, red** 'Go' is an antonym of 'stop' in the same

way as a 'green' traffic light is to a 'red' one.

17 **4** (5 + 4) – (3 + 2) = 4
18 **6** (4 × 3) ÷ 2 = 6
19 **12** (2 × 2) + (3 × 3) – 1 = 12
20 **7** (4 × 1) ÷ 2 + 5 = 7

TEST 21: Mixed (page 22)

1 **fence**
2 **sauce**
3 **muddle**
4 **slice**
5 **water** waterfall, watermark, waterproof, watercolour
6 **fire** firefighter, firework, fireside, firearm
7 **snow** snowman, snowdrop, snowball, snowflake
8 **rain** rainforest, raindrop, raincoat, rainbow
9–12 Arrange the words in a gird to make it easier to put them in the correct alphabetical order.

9 **flatworm**

f	l	a	n	k					1st
f	l	a	n	n	e	l			2nd
f	l	a	t	b	e	d			3rd
f	l	a	t	w	o	r	m		4th
f	l	e	d	g	l	i	n	g	5th

10 **stagnant**

s	t	a	d	i	u	m				1st
s	t	a	g	e	c	o	a	c	h	2nd
s	t	a	g	g	e	r				3rd
s	t	a	g	n	a	n	t			4th
s	t	a	i	n	l	e	s	s		5th

11 **harpoon**

h	a	r	e	l	i	p		1st
h	a	r	m	o	n	i	c	2nd
h	a	r	n	e	s	s		3rd
h	a	r	p	o	o	n		4th
h	a	r	r	i	e	r		5th

12 **largesse**

l	a	p	w	i	n	g		1st
l	a	r	c	e	n	y		2nd
l	a	r	d	e	r			3rd
l	a	r	g	e	s	s	e	4th
l	a	r	v	a				5th

13 **EEL** wheel
14 **AIR** hair
15 **AND** standing
16 **HER** cherries
17 **PI, SF** The first letter moves forward three places. The second letter moves backwards three places.
18 **GF, IH** Both letters move forward two places.
19 **LS, MT** The first letters move forward one place. The second letters are in a repeating pattern in alphabetical order: QQRRSST.
20 **DR, EQ** The first letters are in a repeating pattern in alphabetical order: BBCCDDE. The second letters are in reverse alphabetical order.

TEST 22: Mixed (page 23)

1 **win, lose** Only 'win, lose' are antonyms. The others are synonyms.
2 **warm, cool** 'Warm, cool' are direct opposites as both are neither hot or cold.
3 **clear, cloudy** If a day is 'clear' the sky shows blue. If it is 'cloudy' the sky is obscured.
4 **collect, deliver** 'Collect' is to take something from someone, whereas 'deliver' is to give something to them.
5 **11** (7 × 1) + 3 = 10 and (3 × 5) + 3 = 18, so (4 × 2) + 3 = 11
6 **10** (14 – 4) + 1 = 11 and (13 – 7) + 1 = 7, so (12 – 3) + 1 = 10
7 **5** (5 – 2) × 5 = 15 and (7 – 6) × 5 = 5, so (4 – 3) × 5 = 5
8 **6** (6 + 7) – 5 = 8 and (7 + 4) – 5 = 6, so (8 + 3) – 5 = 6
9 **dart** To 'dart' means to move quickly.
10 **fair** 'Fair' means light in colour; it also means honest or true.
11 **eject** To 'eject' is to throw out, get rid of.
12 **stout** 'Stout' is rounded and fat and well covered rather than light and flimsy.
13 **r** cane, bred
14 **p** light, carp
15 **t** sue, turn
16 **l** food, hilt
17 **SHAPES, PHASES**
18 **GRUNTS, STRUNG**
19 **STAPLE, PALEST**
20 **STALE, LEAST**

TEST 23: Mixed (page 24)

1–5 Category A contains stationery (**rubber, pen**).
Category B contains trees (**beech, pine**).
Category C contains items relating to the coast (**beach, seaweed**).
Category D contains furniture (**bed, chair**).
Category E contains fish (**perch, pike**).

6 **FAME**
7 **HEAT**
8 **PLAN**
9 **CATER**
10 **ADDER**
11 **thick** 'Thin' is skinny or narrow whereas 'thick' is wide or dense.
12 **difficult** 'Easy' is simple whereas 'difficult' is hard.
13 **empty** 'Full' is replete whereas 'empty' has nothing in it.

14 **uneven** 'Flat' is smooth and level whereas 'uneven' is bumpy or cratered.
15 **noisy** 'Quiet' is noiseless whereas 'noisy' is busy and loud.
16 **climb, ascend**
17 **concur, agree**
18 **healthy, well**
19 **arrow, dart**
20 **carpet, rug**

TEST 24: Mixed (page 25)

1 **library, bank** 'Books' are stored in a 'library' as 'money' is stored in a 'bank'.
2 **weekend, weekday** 'Saturday' is a day on the 'weekend' whereas 'Monday' is a working day during the week.
3 **bite, peck** 'Teeth' bite in the same way as birds' beaks 'peck'.
4 **pip, stone** Inside an 'apple' core there are pips in the same way as in the centre of a 'peach' there is a 'stone'.
5 **boat, bicycle** An 'oar' powers a rowing 'boat' in the same way a 'pedal' powers a 'bicycle'.
6 **GAME, SAME**
7 **PLAY, PRAY**
8 **SITE, MITE**
9 **BASH, BATH**
10 **FORK, FORT**
11 **spaceship**
12 **roadworks**
13 **honeycomb**
14 **bullseye**
15 **headlong**
16–20 Use a table to help you work out the information:

Total = 23	Type	Animal	Nationality
4	Soft	Goat	Welsh (2) English (2)
5	Soft	Cow	English (5)
2	Soft	Sheep	English (2)
12	Hard	Cow	Welsh (3) Irish (2) English (7)

16 **11**
17 **soft**
18 **7**
19 **5**
20 **16**

TEST 25: Mixed (page 26)

1 **headstrong, stubborn** Both the words mean inflexible or mulish.
2 **border, edge** Both the words mean rim or perimeter.
3 **edgy, tense** Both words mean nervous or apprehensive.
4 **mutiny, revolt** Both words mean a rebellion.
5 **power, strength** Both words mean control, force or dominance.
6–10 Try each of the words in the first set of brackets. Do they make sense with any words in the second (and sometimes third) set of brackets? Only one combination of words makes sense.
6 **music, radio**
7 **spoke, telephone**
8 **leave, books, teacher**
9 **hippo, rivers, mouth**
10 **brushes, morning, flannel**
11 **DM, HQ** Both letters move forwards one place.
12 **GT, LO** The first letter is moves forwards one place, in alphabetical order. The second letter moves backwards one place, in reverse alphabetical order.
13 **GS, HQ** The first letter is a repeat pattern: FFGGHH. The second letter moves backwards two places.
14 **515, 533** The numbers increase by 9.
15 **10, 23** This is an alternating pattern. The first, third and fifth numbers increase by 3. The second, fourth, sixth and eighth numbers increase by 10.
16 **26, 28** This is an alternating pattern. The first, third and fifth numbers increase by 2. The second, fourth, sixth and eighth numbers increase by 1.
17 **land** landowner, landfill, landlady, landmark
18 **wild** wildlife, wildcat, wildfowl, wildfire
19 **high** highness, highlighter, highlight, highland
20 **wind** windswept, windsurfing, windscreen, windpipe

TEST 26: Mixed (page 27)

1 **s** lass, soak
2 **b** grub, book
3 **n** run, newt
4 **p** cramp, pole
5 **e** kite, else

6–8

P	I	E	C	E
R	■	D	■	A
E	A	G	E	R
E	■	E	■	L
N	O	S	E	Y

9–11

F	L	A	S	H
I	■	N	■	O
R	I	G	H	T
E	■	L	■	E
S	T	E	A	L

12 **Where** did you **put** the car keys?
13 Sam promised to **get** up early in the **morning**.
14 The batsman hit the **ball** over the **pavilion**.
15 He found a **book** he really liked on a **table**.
16 **hero** My uncle says you must take t**he ro**ugh with the smooth.

17 **hall** The teacher was very angry wit**h all** the class.
18 **rest** Mrs Blewitt says they a**re st**ored in her greenhouse.
19 **tall** Mandy has gone to collec**t all** the hockey balls.
20 **here** A young swallow has migrated with t**he re**st of the birds.

TEST 27: Mixed (page 28)

1–3 Make an alphabetical list of the months.

April	June
August	March
December	May
February	November
January	October
July	September

1 **October** 2 **December** 3 **March**

4–7 Use a grid to help you.

B	O	T	T	L	E
A	N	S	S	K	D

Note the relationship between the code and the word 'BOTTLE'. To get from the word to the code, move each letter backwards one place.

4 **ODMBHK** P = O, E = D, N = M, C = B, I = H, L = K
5 **BQZXNM** C = B, R = Q, A = Z, Y = X, O = N, N = M
6 **SPOONS** R = S, O = P, N = O, N = O, M = N, R = S
7 **PLATES** O = P, K = L, Z = A, S = T, D = E, R = S
8 **26 31** The numbers increase by 5.
9 **11, 8** This is an alternating pattern. The first, third, fifth and seventh numbers increase by 1. The second, fourth and sixth numbers also increase by 1.
10 **16, 64** The number doubles each time.
11 **20, 5** This is an alternating pattern. The first, third, fifth and seventh numbers increase by 2. The second, fourth, sixth and eighth numbers decrease by 2.
12 **touch, feel** Both words are describing the senses.
13 **nail, tack** Both words refer to a type of metal fixing, hit by a hammer.
14 **oar, paddle** Both words are a means of powering or manoeuvring a boat.
15 **teacher, instructor** Both words refer to a person who is able to impart knowledge to a student.
16 **blackberry** 17 **armchair** 18 **roundabout**
19 **pillowcase** 20 **hedgerow**

TEST 28: Mixed (page 29)

1 **fair** 'Fair' means impartial as well as yellow- or pale-haired.
2 **right** 'Right' means accurate as well as to repair or make good.
3 **plain** 'Plain' means basic or natural as well as to make obvious and understandable.
4 **rich** 'Rich' means to have a lot of money as well as strong in flavour quite often in an overpowering way.
5 **9** 3 + 2 + 4 = 9
6 **10** (10 ÷ 2) + 5 = 10
7 **6** (3 × 10) ÷ 5 = 6
8 **8** (10 – 3) + (5 – 4) = 8
9 **shot** If you pu**sh ot**her people out of the way, you will be punished.
10 **mean** Ruby's new bike had a black fra**me an**d a white saddle.
11 **test** It takes forty minu**tes t**o cook my lasagne.
12 **tilt** She counted the hours un**til t**he bell rang.
13 **OUR** journey
14 **EAR** beard
15 **TEA** steam
16 **TEN** beaten
17 **swallow** There is only one 'W' in 'PILLOWCASE'.
18 **teacher** There is only one 'E' in 'CHARACTER'.
19 **cross** There is only one 'S' in 'CHROMOSOME'.
20 **noise** There is no 'E' in 'TRANSITION'.

TEST 29: Mixed (page 30)

1 **al** petal, alter
2 **le** handle, hedge
3 **fe** knife, fearless
4 **th** mouth, thorn
5 **PINES** 6 **PLEAT**
7 **CLASP** 8 **TRUST**
9–12 Category A: **Brian, Susan**
Category B: **bus, train**
Category C: **squash, beer**
Category D: **for, under**
13 **azure** 'Azure' is a shade of 'blue'.
14 **tranquil** 'Tranquil' means 'calm' or peaceful.
15 **weep** 'Weep' is to 'cry' or shed tears.
16 **bristle** 'Bristle' is a short length of hair or stem like 'stubble'.
17 **8** When the brother was born, the speaker was 4 and their father 32 (4 × 8). Add 8 years to the father's age, the newborn brother will be 8.
18 **12** The brother is 4 years younger than the speaker. If the speaker is 16, the brother will be 12 (16 – 4).

19 **10** (Z × 2) – 2, then divide by 3 = 6. Work backwards, doing the opposite. 6 × 3 = 18. Then add 2 = 20. Divide 20 by 2 = 10.

20 **13** (Z × 2) – 8, then divide by 3 = 6. Work backwards, doing the opposite. 6 × 3 = 18. Then add 8 = 26. Divide 26 by 2 = 13.

TEST 30: Mixed (page 31)

1–3 Try each of the words in the first set of brackets. Do they make sense with any words in the second and third set of brackets? Only one combination of three words makes sense.

1 **tennis, racquet, court**

2 **goldfish, swam, pondweed**

3 **weather, rainy, ground**

4–8 Mum, Sarah and Tom are next door to each other so they must be 3, 4, 5. If Pete is opposite Tom, then Tom must be 5 and Pete 12. Dad and Sarah are even numbers so Dad 14 and Sarah 4, leaving Mum in 3.

4 **Mum** 5 **Sarah**

6 **Tom** 7 **Pete**

8 **Dad** 9 **grief**

10 **cute** 11 **shake** or **quake**

12 **pride** 13 **trend** 14 **gush**

15–20 Three of the codes start with 9, so 9 = S. 0643 therefore = WANT. 9884 must be SOON. From this you can match all the code numbers to letters.

15 **9064** S = 9, W = 0, A = 6, N = 4

16 **9884** S = 9, O = 8, O = 8, N = 4

17 **0643** W = 0, A = 6, N = 4, T = 3

18 **9480** S = 9, N = 4, O = 8, W = 0

19 **TOWN** 3 = T, 8 = O, 0 = W, 4 = N

20 **ANTS** 6 = A, 4 = N, 3 = T, 9 = S

TEST 31: Mixed (page 32)

1–5 Use grids as shown below to help work out the missing word.

1 **PEAR**

3*		1	2
S	I	Z	E

3*	4		
S	T	U	N

3*		1	2
T	Y	P	E

3*	4		
A	R	C	H

2 **STOP**

		2	1
T	R	I	P

		3/4*	3/4*
T	E	L	L

		2	1
F	A	T	S

		3/4*	3/4*
D	R	O	P

3 **KING**

	2/3*	2/3*	1
S	E	E	R

2/3*		4	
E	N	D	S

	2/3*	2/3*	1
W	I	C	K

2/3*		4	
N	A	G	S

4 **TEAL**

2/3*			1
E	B	B	S

4	2/3*		
N	E	W	T

2/3*			1
E	M	I	T

4	2/3*		
L	A	M	B

5 **SPUR**

	3	2	1
F	E	U	D

4			
T	R	A	M

	3	2	1
C	U	P	S

4			
R	O	U	T

6 **complete, start** To 'start' is to begin whereas 'complete' is to finish.

7 **expose, conceal** 'Expose' is to show whereas 'conceal' is to hide.

8 **distant, approachable** 'Distant' is far away or aloof whereas 'approachable' is closer by and more open-minded.

9 **genuine, fake** 'Genuine' is real whereas 'fake' is a copy or imitation.

10 **praise, criticise** 'Praise' is to commend or approve whereas 'criticise' is to find fault with.

11 **D** A, B and C may or may not be true. They must be rejected because you must only use the information you are given.

12 **8** (10 × 4) ÷ 5 = 8

13 **2** (4 + 3) – (10 – 5) = 2

14 **5** (4 × 5) ÷ 10 + 3 = 5

15 **31** (4 – 3) + (10 × 3) = 31

16 **ACILPST** 17 **ACEMPRS**

18 **ADEIMNRSU** 19 **ABDEKORY** 20 **E**

TEST 32: Mixed (page 33)

1 **f** staff, foxes; cliff, fades

2 **g** stag, glue; frog, greet

3 **n** train, night; toxin, nails

4 **w** jaw, wail; straw, when

5 **evening, morning** 'Dusk' occurs in the 'evening' in the same way 'dawn' occurs in the morning.

6 **navy, ruby** 'Navy' is a shade of 'blue' in the same way 'ruby' is a shade of 'red'.

7 **truth, belief** A 'fact' is a 'truth' in the same way an 'opinion' is a 'belief'.

8 **drop, lower** 'Fall' is a synonym of 'drop' in the same way as 'descend' is a synonym of 'lower'.

9 **WALL, WILL**
10 **TRAP, TRIP**
11 **LIFE, LIME**
12 **SHOT, SOOT**
13 **homework**
14 **eggshell**
15 **backwards**
16 **grandstand**
17 **ankle** These words are all joints in the body.
18 **look** These are all synonyms describing ways of using your eyes and sight.
19 **London** These are all capital cities of Great Britain.
20 **instruct** These are all synonyms meaning to teach.

TEST 33: Mixed (page 34)

1 **EASEL, LEASE**
2 **THROW, WORTH**
3 **SPORE, PROSE**
4 **U\W** Both letters move forward four places. The / becomes \ in the second grouping.
5 **P70** The letters move forward one place. The numbers increase by 5.
6 **v37X** Both sets of letters (lower case and upper case) move forward four places. The numbers increase by 6.
7 **YxW** All the letters move backwards three places.
8 **SR** Both letters move backwards four places.
9 **T – W** Both letters move forwards six places. The + in the first pair becomes – in the second pair.
10 **bed** bedtime, bedclothes, bedroom, bedspread
11 **black** blackboard, blacklist, blackmail, blackbird
12 **life** lifetime, lifelong, lifeblood, lifeless
13 **some** something, someone, somewhere, somewhat
14–16 Try each of the words in the first set of brackets. Do they make sense with any words in the second and third set of brackets? Only one combination of three words makes sense.
14 **hard, banks, road**
15 **bed, pyjamas, hair**
16 **cinema, hurry, film**
17 **i** $(12 \times 5) \div 10 + 4 = 10$ $10 = i$
18 **m** $(10 + 3 + 2) - 12 = 3$ $3 = m$
19 **j** $(4 \times 4) - (2 \times 2) = 12$ $12 = j$
20 **n** $(12 \div 3) - (10 \div 5) = 2$ $2 = n$

TEST 34: Mixed (page 35)

1 **OPQ, WXY** Each letter moves forward four places.
2 **37, 33** This is an alternating pattern. The first, third, fifth and seventh numbers decrease by 11. The second, fourth, sixth and eighth numbers increase by 10.
3 **G24, O48** The letters move forwards two places and alternate between lower case and capital letters. The numbers increase by 6.
4 **10, 15** The number added increases by 1 each time: +3, +4, +5, +6, +7, +8, + 9. So, 6 + 4 = 10, 10 + 5 = 15.
5 **strong** 'Strong' means well developed and strapping and also level and firm.
6 **interior** 'Interior' is the inside of something as well as the very middle, or heart of something.
7 **coach** A 'coach' is a teacher and to 'coach' means to instruct.
8 **interest** An 'interest' could be something that occupies your free time; it can also be the mental quality you direct towards something you want to know about.
9 **listen**
10 **plain**
11 **tracing**
12 **stammer**
13 **AND** handle
14 **OAT** goats
15 **HAM** shampoo
16 **NET** magnetic
17 **c** cash, cart, chart, chair, clap
18 **p** parched, pill, pinched, prim, pale
19 **n** narrow, nearly, neither, neat, nail
20 **o** open, opal, owing, orange, oat

TEST 35: Mixed (page 36)

1 **ASLEEP**
2 **PRIEST**
3 **TRELLIS**
4 **SPADES**
5 **ST<u>R</u>EAM**
6 **<u>S</u>HEARS**
7 **S<u>H</u>ALLOW**
8 **BEL<u>L</u>OW**
9 **crow, clock** The other words all mean a panic or fear.
10 **rubber, ruler** The other words are writing implements.
11 **classroom, teacher** The other words are school subjects.
12 **cube, pyramid** The other words are two-dimensional shapes.
13 **four, three** A 'chair' has 'four' legs whereas a 'stool' has 'three' legs.
14 **scales, fur** 'Fish' have 'scales' in the same way a 'bear' has 'fur'.
15 **lid, roof** A 'lid' is the top or covering of a 'box' in the same way a 'roof' is the top or covering of the house.
16 **drive, beach** A 'drive' may be covered in 'gravel' in the same way a 'beach' may be covered in 'sand'.
17–20 Identify the first six letters of the alphabet: ABCDEF.
17 **efface**
18 **added**
19 **faced**
20 **dead**

TEST 36: Mixed (page 37)

1–4 Use a grid to help you.

C	H	R	I	S	T	M	A	S
*	!	/	%	?	\	£	:	?

1 **? ! % / ** S = ?, H = !, I = %, R = /, T = \\
2 **£ : / * !** M = £, A = :, R = /, C = *, H = !
3 **STRICT** ? = S, \\ = T, / = R, % = I, * = C, \\ = T
4 **ASSIST** : = A, ? = S, ? = S, % = I, ? = S, \\ = T

5–6 Use a grid to help you. Look carefully at the relationship between the letters and their number codes. Note that A = 1, B = 2, D = 4. Therefore, the numbers must correlate with the alphabetical places, eg C = 3, Z = 26 etc.

D	A	B	B	L	E
4	1	2	2	12	5

5 **3 1 2 12 5** C = 3, A = 1, B = 2, L = 12, E = 5
6 **6 1 3 5 4** F = 6, A = 1, C = 3, E = 5, D = 4

7–9

C	L	A	I	M	S
R		L			T
A	R	M	O	U	R
D		O			O
L		N			N
E	N	D	I	N	G

10–12

B	U	S	T	L	E
O		U		A	
U	D	D	E	R	S
N		D		G	
D	E	E	P	E	R
S		N		R	

13 **your** Dad asked me if I knew why our radio was broken.
14 **rent** My aunt took her children to the theme park.
15 **stem** Deborah's temper got the better of her in class.
16 **done** The police raided one address in Birmingham.

17–20 Draw a diagram to help you.

Bourne	North	Ashley
West		East
Dalton	South	Calne

17 **Bourne** 18 **Dalton**
19 **south** 20 **south-east**

TEST 37: Mixed (page 38)

1 **PLAY, SLAY** 2 **TYRE, TORE**
3 **CLOP, CROP** 4 **FOUL, FOOL**
5 **b** brain, blend, brake, beast, band
6 **l** lend, lout, lever, learn, lawful
7 **a** ascent, amaze, awake, ashore, ajar
8 **g** glad, gorge, gamble, glisten, grange
9 **MN** The first letter moves forwards five places. The second letter moves backwards five places.
10 **UWZ** Each of the letters moves forwards seven places.
11 **caterpillar, leaf** A 'butterfly' drinks 'nectar' as a 'caterpillar' eats a 'leaf'.
12 **fast, hare** A 'tortoise' moves slowly as a 'hare' moves 'fast'.
13 **I28** The letters move backwards three places. The numbers increase by 3.
14 **; / $ @** The symbols are reversed in the second grouping.
15 **gun, bullet** An 'arrow' is fired from a 'bow' as a 'bullet' is fired from a 'gun'.
16 **time, clock** 'Speed' is measured on a 'speedometer' as 'time' is measured on a 'clock'.
17 **Sally** feeds her **guinea-pigs** every day before breakfast.
18 For lunch today, we had roast **chicken** followed by fruit **salad**.
19 I am **finding** my **maths** homework hard.
20 My favourite **television** programme **starts** at 8.00pm.

TEST 38: Mixed (page 39)

1 **plate** The pattern is to remove the last letter from the first word and replace it with 'te'.
2 **plant** The pattern is to remove the third, fourth and fifth letters of the first word.
3 **rout** The pattern is to remove the 'a' from the first word and replaced it with 'ou' in the second word.
4 **bug** The pattern is to remove the middle 'd' and the final 'e' from the first word.
5 **blown** The pattern is two replace the first two letters of the first word, 'fr', with 'bl' in the second word.
6 **narrow** 'Short' and 'tall' are antonyms. The opposite of 'wide' is 'narrow'.
7 **over** 'Through' and 'around' are antonyms. The opposite of 'under' is 'over'.
8 **speak** 'Chatter', 'babble' are synonyms, as are 'talk' and 'speak'
9 **illuminate** 'Delicate' and 'flimsy' are synonyms. 'Light' and 'illuminate' are also synonyms.
10 **fasten** 'Laces' are 'tied' in the same way as 'buttons' are 'fastened'.

11 **40, 24** This is an alternating pattern. The first, third, fifth and seventh numbers decrease by 5. The second, fourth, sixth and eighth numbers increase by 4.

12 **11, 10** This is an alternating pattern. The first, third, fifth and seventh numbers increase by 3. The second, fourth, sixth and eighth numbers also increase by 3.

13 **t18, v31** The letters move forward one place. The number added increases by 1 each time: +2, +3, +4, +5, +6, +7, +8.

14 **GIT, HJS** The first two letters move forward one place. The third letter moves backwards one place.

15 **EHf, CFd** All the letters move forwards four places.

16–20 Use grids as shown below to help work out the missing word.

16 **MOAT**

		2	1
S	P	O	T

	3		4
R	A	I	D

		2	1
B	O	O	M

	3		4
S	A	L	T

17 **DRIP**

	3	2	1
C	A	T	S

4			
B	I	L	E

	3	2	1
B	I	R	D

4			
P	I	N	K

18 **RAID**

4*		2	1*
T	R	I	P

1*		3	4*
P	A	N	T

4*		2	1*
F	E	A	R

1*		3	4*
G	R	I	D

19 **TAIL**

	4	2/3*	1
S	L	O	W

	2/3*		
P	O	S	H

	4	2/3*	1
S	L	A	T

	2/3*		
K	I	L	L

20 **DEAL**

4	2*	3	1*
T	E	A	M

1*			2*
M	I	L	E

4	2*	3	1*
L	E	A	F

1*			2*
D	I	C	E

TEST 39: Mixed (page 40)

1–5 Use a table to help you.

	Naomi	Fern	Husna	Debra
Spanish	✓	✓	✓	
French		✓	✓	✓
Art	✓		✓	✓
Chemistry	✓	✓		✓
Greek			✓	
Geography		✓		✓
Textiles	✓			✓
Music		✓	✓	

1 **Fern** 2 **Naomi** 3 **Husna**

4 **Debra** 5 **Naomi**

6–9 Use a grid to help you. Look carefully at the relationship between the letters and codes. To get from the word 'CANDLE' to the code, move each letter forwards two places.

C	A	N	D	L	E
E	C	P	F	N	G

6 **NKIJV** L = N, I = K, G = I, H = J, T = V

7 **FCTMPGUU** D = F, A = C, R = T, K = M, N = P, E = G, S = U, S = U

8 **LUCKY** N = L, W = U, E = C, M = K, A = Y

9 **CRAZY** E = C, R = T, A = C, Z = B, Y = A

10 **rigid, sturdy** These words are all synonyms and all mean much the same.

11 **defeat, conquer** These words are all synonyms and all mean much the same.

12 **inaccurate, false** These words are antonyms. The opposite of 'true' is 'false'.

13 **firm, harsh** 'Hard' and 'firm' are synonyms in the same way as are 'coarse' and 'harsh'.

14 **proud, arrogant** These words are antonyms. 'Modest' and 'humble' are the opposites of 'proud' and 'arrogant'.

15 **ADGHRTU** 16 **CEMOPRTU**

17 **DRAWL, DRAWN, DREAM**

18 **HEARTH, HEARTY, HEATER**

19 **Saturday** Friday, Monday, Saturday, Sunday, Thursday, Tuesday, Wednesday

20 **R**

TEST 40: Mixed (page 41)

1 **12, 12** This is an alternating pattern. The first, third, fifth and seventh numbers increase by 6. The second, fourth, sixth and eighth numbers decrease by 3.

2 **ZAB, YBC** The first letter moves backwards one place. The second and third letters move forward one place.

3 **15b, 11a** The number subtracted decreases by 1 each time: −10, −9, −8, −7, −6, −5, −4. The letters move backwards one place.
4 **RSq, ZAy** All the letters move forwards four places.
5 **WORD, WARD**
6 **ROSE, RISE**
7 **LAZE, LAME**
8 **RICE, RISE**
9 **PURE, SURE**
10 **BEAT, BOAT**
11 **FLEA, FLEW**
12 **HOME, HOSE**
13 **w** wheel, what, wall, whale, weighty
14 **h** height, herring, heel, hedge, hearth
15 **p** potter, park, plight, phoney, prattle
16 **e** elope, eat, ebony, estate, event
17–20 From the information you know that Gretel is at the side of the theatre, therefore 2J. If Sandra sat directly three rows behind Pravin, then she must be in 4D and Pravin in 1D. Clement sits next to Pravin, therefore Clement = 1C. If Penelope sits diagonally in front of Sandra (4D) the Penelope = 3E. Judy sits next to her sister. Therefore, her sister must be Sandra (4D) so Judy = 4E. If Harold is closer to Kang rather than anyone else, he must be in 2G which would leave space around him, leaving Kang in 2F.
1C = Clement
1D = Pravin
2F = Kang
2G = Harold
2J = Gretel
3E = Penelope
4D = Sandra
4E = Judy

Puzzle 1 (page 42)

1–4 The key here is to look at the end of the words. Find a word that ends with a letter that is also at the beginning of a word. Once you have established those two words, you can place all of them.

1

P	R	I	Z	E
R	■	N	■	N
I	N	L	E	T
Z	■	L	■	E
E	N	T	E	R

2

A	W	A	R	E
W	■	C	■	N
A	C	R	I	D
R	■	I	■	E
E	N	D	E	D

3

S	A	L	T	S
A	■	I	■	T
L	I	V	E	R
T	■	E	■	A
S	T	R	A	P

4

B	A	T	O	N
A	■	A	■	E
T	A	U	P	E
O	■	P	■	D
N	E	E	D	S

5–10 Look at the first letters of all the words. Rearrange them to make one of the words. You will now have found the first word across and down.

5

M	E	A	T
E	A	C	H
A	C	H	E
T	H	E	N

6

D	A	I	S
A	U	N	T
I	N	T	O
S	T	O	P

7

P	R	A	Y
R	A	R	E
A	R	E	A
Y	E	A	R

8

S	I	G	N
I	D	E	A
G	E	R	M
N	A	M	E

9

E	A	G	E	R
A	L	O	N	E
G	O	U	D	A
E	N	D	E	D
R	E	A	D	S

10

S	T	A	M	P
T	H	R	E	E
A	R	E	A	S
M	E	A	N	T
P	E	S	T	O

Puzzle 2 (page 43)

Look at the clues and solve as many as you can. Position them on the lily pads so that one letter is altered each time. If you cannot work out the word looking at the clue, go to the lily pads and replace one letter at a time to make a new word and see if you can identify the clues.

1 PARK, PACK, SACK
2 BELT, BEST, BUST
3 MOAN, MOON, MOOR
4 PINT, MINT, MIST
5 CROW, BROW, BLOW

Puzzle 3 (page 44)

Fill in the grid with crosses as well as ticks as you go through the information.
You know that Grandpa was with a girl, so put a cross for James against Grandpa and one for Jamila and donkey rides. A tick for Clare for the ice creams and crosses for all the other options, as well as crosses for the other children and ice creams. You can also put a cross for Clare and Grandpa and Grandpa and ice creams. Learn that James was with his big sister, so tick for him and crosses for the others. Finally, you know Mum had fun playing beach games, so that can't be Clare or James as well. Put in the ticks and crosses and you will be able to deduce all the rest of the grid.
Ice creams must be Clare and her aunt. Put in the ticks and crosses and you can solve the grid.

	mum	grandpa	aunt	sister	funfair	donkey ride	ice cream	beach games
Lucy	×	✓	×	×	×	✓	×	×
Clare	×	×	✓	×	×	×	✓	×
James	×	×	×	✓	✓	×	×	×
Jamila	✓	×	×	×	×	×	×	✓
funfair	×	×	×	✓				
donkey ride	×	✓	×	×				
ice cream	×	×	✓	×				
beach games	✓	×	×	×				

	RELATIVE	TREAT
Lucy	grandpa	donkey ride
Clare	aunt	ice cream
James	sister	funfair
Jamila	mum	beach games

Puzzle 4 (page 45)

Look at the length of the words you have to fit into the grid. For example, if there is only one word of 8 letters long and only one space big enough, you can place that word. Once you have looked at that and exhausted the possibilities, look at your downwards space and see where the letters intersect the other horizontal words. Pick out the appropriate letters of those words. Are they likely to go next to each other in the downwards word? If not, try another one.

1 water
2 eating
3 sentence

Puzzle 5 (page 46)

Blend the consonants together and work round each of the letters in turn. When you have made one word, use it to rhyme other words (for example: late, sate, pate) or use the letters again in another order (for example: late, tale, teal). Try taking it in turns with the different letters and put different endings on them (for example: sea, set, sap, sat). To get longer words, think of the shape of the words, blending the consonants (pleat), splitting up the vowels (paste), putting the vowels together (least), making plurals with your 's' and so on.
Possible answers include:
6-letter: staple, pastel, petals, plates, pleats, palest
5-letter: stale, steal, tales, plate, pleas, slept, pleat, least, pelts, slate, splat, lapse, petal, pales
4-letter: last, salt, plea, slap, slat, pale, sale, late, tale, leap, seal, peal, pelt, lets, leas
3-letter: let, lap, pal, ale, lea

TEST 24: Mixed

Test time: 0 5 10 minutes

Complete the following sentences in the best way by choosing one word from each set of brackets.

Example Tall is to (tree, <u>short</u>, colour) as narrow is to (thin, white, <u>wide</u>).

1 Book is to (library, author, paper) as money is to (cash, bank, exchange).

2 Saturday is to (weekend, supermarket, holiday) as Monday is to (washing, weekday, school).

3 Tooth is to (bite, filling, mouth) as beak is to (nest, worms, peck).

4 Apple is to (wine, juice, pip) as peach is to (apricot, stone, tree).

5 Oar is to (mine, ship, boat) as pedal is to (bicycle, horse, pushers).

Change the first word into the last word by changing one letter at a time, and making two new, different words in the middle.

Example CASE CASH WASH WISH

6 GATE ________ ________ SOME

7 PLAN ________ ________ PREY

8 SIZE ________ ________ MUTE

9 BASK ________ ________ BOTH

10 WORK ________ ________ FONT

Underline two words, one from each group, that go together to form a new word. The word in the first group always comes first.

Example (hand, <u>green</u>, for) (light, <u>house,</u> sure)

11 (old, space, fishing) (age, ship, boat)

12 (road, lane, street) (works, stop, gear)

13 (darling, honey, hare) (brush, hive, comb)

14 (pigs, bulls, birds) (eye, ear, nose)

15 (bread, stick, head) (short, long, wide)

From the information supplied, answer the questions.

There were 23 different types of cheese on a cheese counter at the farm shop.
There were four different types of soft goats' cheese, two of these were Welsh, the rest English.
There were seven other types of soft cheese; five cows' cheeses and two cheeses made from milk taken from sheep. All these were English.
There were 12 hard cows' cheeses, three from Wales and two from Ireland.

16 How many soft cheeses were there? ________

17 Are the sheep's cheeses soft or hard? ________

18 How many English hard cheeses were there? ________

19 How many Welsh cheeses were there altogether? ________

20 How many English cheeses were there altogether? ________

Time for a break! Go to Puzzle Page 44

Total

TEST 25: Mixed

Test time: 0 5 10 minutes

Underline the two words, one from each group, that are closest in meaning.

Example (race, shop, start) (finish, begin, end)

1 (headlong, headstrong, headline) (stubborn, lengthy, mark)
2 (clothes, line, border) (flower, straight, edge)
3 (edgy, calm, sensible) (tender, tense, hectic)
4 (pirate, mutiny, crew) (revolt, repulse, revive)
5 (power, tower, mower) (length, width, strength)

Complete the following sentences by selecting the most sensible word from each group of words given in the brackets. Underline the words selected.

Example The (children, boxes, foxes) carried the (houses, books, steps) home from the (greengrocer, library, factory).

6 My aunt listens to (music, tortoises, trees) on the (bathroom, radio, dustbin).
7 I (spoke, saw, ran) to Jo on the (television, park, telephone).
8 "Kindly (eat, leave, climb) those (tomatoes, stairs, books) alone!" shouted the (desk, teacher, goldfish).
9 A (hippo, giraffe, mouse) lives mostly in African (rivers, houses, airports) and has a big (ear, mouth, neck).
10 Before Adam (combs, counts, brushes) his teeth in the (classroom, morning, jungle) he likes to wash his face with his (flannel, hairbrush, dog).

A B C D E F G H I J K L M N O P Q R S T U V W X Y Z

Give the two missing groups of letters or numbers in the following sequences. The alphabet has been written out to help you.

Example CQ DP EQ FP GQ HP

11 CL ___ EN FO GP ___
12 ___ HS IR JQ KP ___
13 FY FW GU ___ ___ HO
14 506 ___ 524 ___ 542 551
15 17 ___ 20 20 ___ 30 26 40
16 24 25 ___ 26 28 27 30 ___

Find a word that can be put in front of each of the following words to make a new, compound word.

Example cast fall ward pour down

17 owner fill lady mark ___
18 life cat fowl fire ___
19 ness lighter light land ___
20 swept surfing screen pipe ___

Total

Test 26: Mixed

Test time: 0 5 10 minutes

Find the letter which will end the first word and start the second word.

Example peac (h) ome

1 las (_) oak **2** gru (_) ook **3** ru (_) ewt

4 cram (_) ole **5** kit (_) lse

Fill in the crosswords so that all the words are included.

6–8

EARLY NOSEY

EAGER PREEN

PIECE EDGES

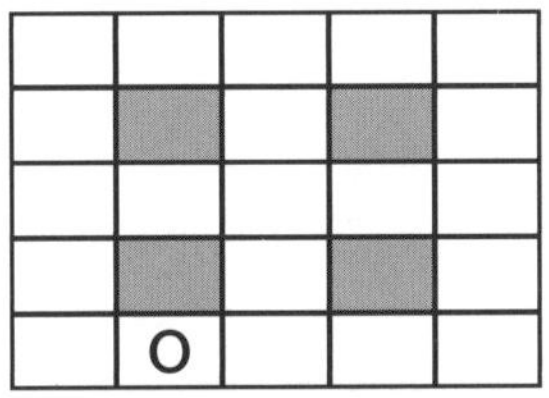

9–11

STEAL FLASH

HOTEL FIRES

ANGLE RIGHT

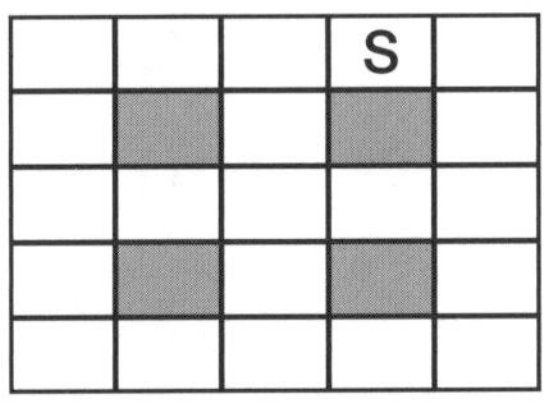

Find and underline the two words that need to change places for each sentence to make sense.

Example She went to letter the write.

12 Put did you where the car keys?

13 Sam promised to morning up early in the get.

14 The batsman hit the pavilion over the ball.

15 He found a table he really liked on a book.

Write the four-letter word hidden at the end of one word and the beginning of the next word. The order of the letters may not be changed.

Example We had bats and balls. sand

16 My uncle says you must take the rough with the smooth. ______

17 The teacher was very angry with all the class. ______

18 Mrs Blewitt says they are stored in her greenhouse. ______

19 Mandy has gone to collect all the hockey balls. ______

20 A young swallow has migrated with the rest of the birds. ______

Total

TEST 27: Mixed

Test time: 0 5 10 minutes

If the months were put in alphabetical order, which would be:

1 the second last month? ____________

2 the third month? ____________

3 the month after June? ____________

A B C D E F G H I J K L M N O P Q R S T U V W X Y Z

The word BOTTLE is written in code as ANSSKD. Encode each of these words using the same code.

4 PENCIL ____________ 5 CRAYON ____________

Decode these words using the same code as above.

6 RONNMR ____________ 7 OKZSDR ____________

Give the two missing numbers in the following sequences.

Example	CQ	DP	EQ	FP	GQ	HP		
8	___	___	36	41	46	51		
9	5	9	6	10	7	___	___	
10	4	8	___	32	___	128		
11	16	9	18	7	___	___	22	3

Underline two words from the group which are most similar in type or meaning.

Example	<u>dear</u>	pleasant	poor	extravagant	<u>expensive</u>
12	touch	feel	smoke	laugh	ring
13	hammer	nail	finger	tack	varnish
14	coal	gem	oar	majesty	paddle
15	neighbour	teacher	friend	niece	instructor

Underline two words, one from each group, that go together to form a new word. The word in the first group always comes first.

Example	(hand, <u>green</u>, for)	(light, <u>house</u>, sure)
16	(sea, green, black)	(berry, current, piece)
17	(turn, right, arm)	(gate, stop, chair)
18	(ground, round, water)	(under, about, place)
19	(pillow, briefs, picnic)	(place, case, sheet)
20	(vegetable, grass, hedge)	(wood, green, row)

Total

TEST 28: **Mixed**

Test time: 0 5 10 minutes

Underline one word in brackets that will go equally well with both pairs of words outside the brackets.

Example	rush, attack	cost, fee	(price, hasten, strike, charge, money)
1	just, equal	blonde, light	(fair, plus, yellow, appropriate, true)
2	correct, precise	fix, mend	(exact, wrong, right, sum, sort)
3	undecorated, simple	clear, direct	(easy, ugly, flat, plain, straight)
4	wealthy, affluent	unhealthy, creamy	(satisfactory, well, rich, correctly, strong)

If a = 2, b = 5, c = 4, d = 3 and e = 10, find the value of the following.

5 $d + a + c =$ _____ **6** $\frac{e}{a} + b =$ _____ **7** $\frac{de}{b} =$ _____ **8** $(e - d) + (b - c) =$ _____

Write the four-letter word hidden at the end of one word and the beginning of the next word. The order of the letters may not be changed.

Example We had bats and balls. sand

9 If you push other people out of the way, you will be punished. __________

10 Ruby's new bike had a black frame and a white saddle. __________

11 It takes forty minutes to cook my lasagne. __________

12 She counted the hours until the bell rang. __________

Find the three-letter word that can be added to the letters in capitals to make a new word. The new word will complete the sentence sensibly. Write the three-letter word.

Example The cat sprang onto the MO. USE

13 The JNEY to Scotland took a long time. __________

14 The old man had a long grey BD. __________

15 Don't burn yourself on the SM from the kettle. __________

16 The BEA finalist congratulated the winner. __________

Underline the one word in each group that cannot be made from the letters of the word in capital letters.

Example	STATIONERY	stone	tyres	ration	nation	noisy
17	PILLOWCASE	swallow	lapse	scalp	callow	scale
18	CHARACTER	crater	charter	earth	teacher	reach
19	CHROMOSOME	choose	morose	chrome	rooms	cross
20	TRANSITION	artist	nations	noise	strait	station

Total

Test 29: Mixed

Test time: 0 5 10 minutes

Find two letters that will end the first word and start the second word.

Example pas (t a) ste

1 pet (__ __) ter

2 hand (__ __) dge

3 kni (__ __) arless

4 mou (__ __) orn

Rearrange the letters in capitals to make another word. The new word has something to do with the first two words or phrases.

Example spot soil SAINT STAIN

5	longs for	yearns	SNIPE	________
6	fold	crease	PETAL	________
7	clutch	pin part of a brooch	SCALP	________
8	faith	belief	STRUT	________

Look at these words. Sort them into groups.

9–12 Brian bus for train under squash Susan beer

A Names	B Transport	C Drinks	D Prepositions
________	________	________	________
________	________	________	________

Underline the word in brackets closest in meaning to the word in capitals.

Example UNHAPPY (unkind, death, laughter, sad, friendly)

13 BLUE (pink, bruise, sky, downfall, azure)

14 CALM (lake, rough, kind, tranquil, stormy)

15 CRY (whisper, weep, call, say, tearful)

16 STUBBLE (chin, field, straw, bristle, fall)

From the information supplied, complete the statements.

I was 4 when my brother was born. My father was 8 times older than I was then.

17 When my father is 40 my brother will be ________ years old.

18 When I am 16, my brother will be ________ years old.

From the information supplied, answer the questions.

Z is a number. Double it and take away 2. Divide by 3 and the answer is 6.

19 What is Z? ________

20 What would Z be if you take away 8 instead of 2? ________

Total

TEST 30: **Mixed**

Test time: 0 5 10 minutes

Complete the following sentences by selecting the most sensible word from each group of words given in the brackets. Underline the words selected.

Example The (children, boxes, foxes) carried the (houses, books, steps) home from the (greengrocer, library, factory).

1 The (tennis, football, golf) player lifted his (club, racquet, shirt) and hit the ball into the (yard, goal, court).

2 The (banana, goldfish, man) (swam, climbed, lay) around the bowl amongst the (pondweed, kitchen, salad).

3 The weather forecaster said the (rain, weather, cloud) would be (weather, rainy, map) this afternoon with snow on high (ground, tea, cloud).

From the information supplied, answer the questions.

A family went to the swimming baths and put their clothes in different lockers.
Mum, Sarah and Tom put their clothes in lockers next door to each other.
Pete put his in the locker opposite Tom's. Dad and Sarah used even numbered lockers.
The unavailable lockers are shaded. Who used which locker?

4 Locker 3 ____________

5 Locker 4 ____________

6 Locker 5 ____________

7 Locker 12 ____________

8 Locker 14 ____________

1	2	3	4	5	6	7
8	9	10	11	12	13	14

Find a word that is similar in meaning to the word in capital letters and that rhymes with the second word.

Example CABLE tyre wire

9 MISERY beef ____________ 10 PRETTY suit ____________

11 QUIVER brake ____________ 12 CONCEIT wide ____________

13 FASHION friend ____________ 14 POUR thrush ____________

Here are the number codes for four words.
9480 0643 9064 9884
Match the right code to the right word.

15 SWAN ________ 16 SOON ________ 17 WANT ________ 18 SNOW ________

Decode these words using the same code as above.

19 3804 ________ 20 6439 ________

Total

TEST 31: **Mixed**

Test time: 0 5 10 minutes

Look at the first group of three words. The word in the middle has been made from the two other words. Complete the second group of three words in the same way, making a new word in the middle of the group.

Example	PAIN	INTO	TOOK	ALSO	SOON	ONLY
1	SIZE	ZEST	STUN	TYPE	________	ARCH
2	TRIP	PILL	TELL	FATS	________	DROP
3	SEER	REED	ENDS	WICK	________	NAGS
4	EBBS	SEEN	NEWT	EMIT	________	LAMB
5	FEUD	DUET	TRAM	CUPS	________	ROUT

Underline the two words, one from each group, which are the most opposite in meaning.

Example (dawn, early, wake) (late, stop, sunrise)

6 (complete, compete, compel) (entire, start, win)

7 (hide, expose, cruise) (depose, conceal, decrease)

8 (stately, friendly, distant) (approachable, anger, dislike)

9 (dead, genuine, alive) (real, blunt, fake)

10 (praise, practise, prance) (criticise, compliment, commend)

From the information supplied, underline the one statement below it that must be true.

11 Sheena was given a pot plant. It was not watered so it died.

A The plant was a birthday present.
C Sheena liked plants.
B Sheena was too busy to water the plant.
D The plant needed water to stay alive.

If a = 10, b = 4, c = 3 and d = 5, find the value of the following.

12 $\frac{ab}{d}$ = ___ **13** (b + c) − (a − d) = ___ **14** $\frac{bd}{a}$ + c = ___ **15** (b − c) + ac = ___

Write the letters in the following words in alphabetical order.

16 PLASTIC ____________ **17** SCAMPER ____________

18 NURSEMAID ____________ **19** KEYBOARD ____________

From the information supplied answer the question.

I appear twice in INNUMERABLE, once in SINCE and not at all in NATIONAL.

20 Which letter is being described? ___

Total

TEST 32: Mixed

Test time: 0 5 10 minutes

Find the one letter that will end the first word and start the second word of each pair of words. The same letter must be used for both pairs of words.

Example mea (t) able fi (t) ab

1	staf (___) oxes	clif (___) ades	**2**	sta (___) lue	fro (___) reet
3	trai (___) ight	toxi (___) ails	**4**	ja (___) ail	stra (___) hen

Complete the following sentences in the best way by choosing one word from each set of brackets.

Example Tall is to (tree, short, colour) as narrow is to (thin, white, wide).

5 Dusk is to (sunset, evening, dark) as dawn is to (beginning, hours, morning).

6 Blue is to (sky, black, navy) as red is to (orange, blood, ruby).

7 Fact is to (truth, guess, idea) as opinion is to (proof, evidence, belief).

8 Fall is to (drop, water, autumn) as descend is to (lower, raise, winter).

Change the first word into the last word by changing one letter at a time, and making two new, different words in the middle.

Example CASE CASH WASH WISH

9	WALK	______	______	PILL	**10**	TRAY	______	______	DRIP
11	LIFT	______	______	LAME	**12**	SHOE	______	______	BOOT

Underline two words, one from each group, that go together to form a new word. The word in the first group always comes first.

Example (hand, green, for) (light, house, sure)

13 (home, guest, hotel) (going, work, bill)

14 (yolk, egg, soup) (plate, pudding, shell)

15 (back, drake, lever) (let, wards, for)

16 (low, high, grand) (sit, stand, seat)

Underline the word in the brackets which goes best with the words given outside the brackets.

Example word, paragraph, sentence (pen, cap, letter, top, stop)

17 elbow, shoulder, knee (leg, arm, ankle, head, body)

18 peek, glance, peep (mountain, sight, stare, eyes, look)

19 Belfast, Edinburgh, Cardiff (Athens, Dublin, England, London, Iceland)

20 coach, train, drill (engine, instruct, tool, man, rails)

Total

Time for a break! Go to Puzzle Page 45

TEST 33: Mixed

Test time: 0 5 10 minutes

Underline the two words that are made from the same letters.

Example TAP PET TEA POT EAT

1	EASEL	LEAST	SLATS	LEASE	STEEL
2	WORST	WRATH	THROW	WORTH	THREW
3	RASPS	SPORE	SPARE	PROSE	SPOON

A B C D E F G H I J K L M N O P Q R S T U V W X Y Z

Fill in the missing letters, symbols or numbers.

Example AB is to CD as PQ is to RS.

4 A/C is to E\G as Q/S is to ______.

5 G25 is to H30 as O65 is to ______.

6 f14H is to j20L as r31T is to ______.

7 HgF is to EdC as BaZ is to ______.

8 LK is to HG as WV is to ______.

9 M+P is to S – V as N+Q is to ______.

Find a word that can be put in front of each of the following words to make a new, compound word.

Example cast fall ward pour down

10	time	clothes	room	spread	______
11	board	list	mail	bird	______
12	time	long	blood	less	______
13	thing	one	where	what	______

Complete the following sentences by selecting the most sensible word from each group of words given in the brackets. Underline the words selected.

Example The (children, boxes, foxes) carried the (houses, books, steps) home from the (greengrocer, library, factory).

14 It was raining so (soft, slowly, hard) that the river burst its (banks, balloons, beds) and flooded the (crowd, road, river).

15 Before going to (school, church, bed) at night, Tracey puts on her (pyjamas, anorak, skis) and brushes her (shoes, carpets, hair).

16 We arrived late at the (cinema, ferry, shop) so had to (eat, rest, hurry) to see the beginning of the (book, film, concert).

If i = 10, j = 12, k = 4, l = 5, m = 3 and n = 2, find the value of the following. Write your answers as letters.

17 $\frac{jl}{i} + k =$ ______

18 $(i + m + n) - j =$ ______

19 $k^2 - n^2 =$ ______

20 $\frac{j}{m} - \frac{i}{l} =$ ______

Total

TEST 34: **Mixed**

Test time: 0 5 10 minutes

A B C D E F G H I J K L M N O P Q R S T U V W X Y Z

Give the two missing groups of letters and numbers in the following sequences. The alphabet has been written out to help you.

Example CQ DP EQ FP GQ HP

1	GHI	KLM	____	STU	____	ABC		
2	66	17	55	27	44	____	____	47
3	a6	C12	e18	____	i30	K36	m42	____
4	3	6	____	____	21	28	36	45

Underline one word in brackets that will go equally well with both pairs of words outside the brackets.

Example rush, attack cost, fee (price, hasten, strike, charge, money)

5 muscular, powerful solid, stable (frozen, strong, long-lasting, consistent, melted)

6 inner, inside centre, core (interior, inland, exterior, indoors, island)

7 instructor, tutor teach, drill (scout, bus, coach, student, learn)

8 hobby, activity attention, curiosity (interview, interfere, interest, intercept, intern)

Underline the one word in each group that can be made from the letters of the word in capital letters.

Example CHAMPION camping notch peach cramp chimp

9	NESTLING	guest	slings	stink	gentle	listen
10	PINEAPPLE	ample	pliant	plain	planet	ripple
11	SCRATCHING	grate	tracing	strings	crouch	search
12	MAINSTREAM	straits	stammer	monster	strains	matter

Find the three-letter word that can be added to the letters in capitals to make a new word. The new word will complete the sentence sensibly. Write the three-letter word.

Example The cat sprang onto the MO. USE

13 The door HLE has broken. ________

14 We have lots of GS on our farm. ________

15 The bottle of SPOO is in the bathroom. ________

16 Some metals are MAGIC. ________

Which one letter can be added to the front of all of these words to make new words?

Example care cat crate call clip

17 __ash __art __hart __hair __lap

18 __arched __ill __inch __rim __ale

19 __arrow __early __either __eat __ail

20 __pen __pal __wing __range __at

Total

TEST 35: Mixed

Test time: 0 5 10 minutes

Rearrange the letters in capitals to make another word. The new word has something to do with the first two words or phrases.

Example	spot	soil	SAINT	STAIN
1	inattentive	not awake	PLEASE	________
2	preacher	holy man	STRIPE	________
3	framework	support for plants	TILLERS	________
4	suit in cards	digging tools	PASSED	________

Add one letter to the word in capital letters to make a new word. The meaning of the new word is given in the clue.

Example	PLAN	simple	PLAIN
5	STEAM	a small river	________
6	HEARS	a cutting tool	________
7	SALLOW	not deep	________
8	BELOW	to shout	________

Underline the two words that are the odd ones out in each group of words.

Example	black	<u>king</u>	purple	green	<u>house</u>
9	scare	crow	fright	shock	clock
10	pencil	rubber	ruler	pen	biro
11	history	geography	biology	classroom	teacher
12	cube	triangle	square	pyramid	rectangle

Complete the following sentences in the best way by choosing one word from each set of brackets.

Example Tall is to (tree, <u>short</u>, colour) as narrow is to (thin, white, <u>wide</u>).

13 Chair is to (four, six, two) as stool is to (kitchen, three, legs).

14 Fish is to (water, fin, scales) as bear is to (cub, fur, honey).

15 Box is to (cardboard, lid, label) as house is to (roof, chimney, upstairs).

16 Gravel is to (drive, stone, grey) as sand is to (castle, beach, Blackpool).

Underline any words below that contain only the first six letters of the alphabet.

17	coffee	beach	efface	dabble	dance
18	pebble	back	clubs	basin	added
19	fiction	freckle	fatigue	fudge	faced
20	abacus	dead	dread	cradle	adding

Total

Test 36: **Mixed**

Test time: 0 5 10 minutes

The code for the word CHRISTMAS is *!/%?\£:?. Encode each of these words using the same code.

1 SHIRT ____________ **2** MARCH ____________

Decode these words using the same code as above.

3 ?\/%*\ ____________ **4** :??%?\ ____________

The code for the word DABBLE is 4 1 2 2 12 5. Encode each of these words using the same code.

5 CABLE ____________ **6** FACED ____________

Fill in the crosswords so that all the words are included.

7–9

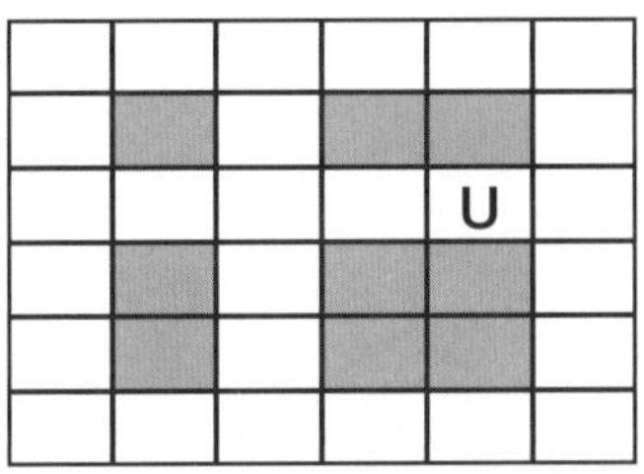

CLAIMS STRONG ARMOUR

ENDING ALMOND CRADLE

10–12

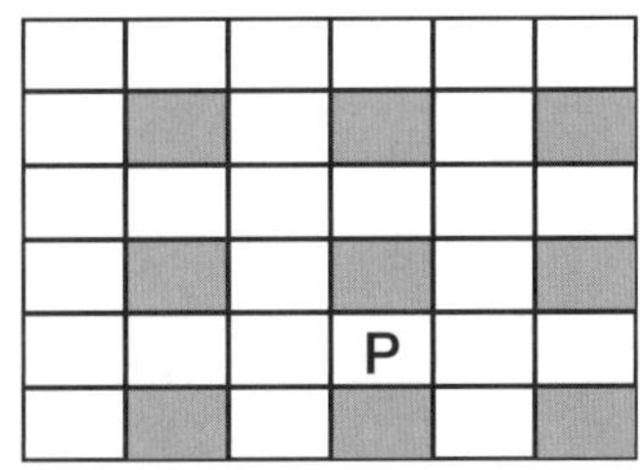

DEEPER LARGER BOUNDS

SUDDEN UDDERS BUSTLE

Write the four-letter word hidden at the end of one word and the beginning of the next word. The order of the letters may not be changed.

Example We had bat<u>s and</u> balls. sand

13 Dad asked me if I knew why our radio was broken. ____________

14 My aunt took her children to the theme park. ____________

15 Deborah's temper got the better of her in class. ____________

16 The police raided one address in Birmingham. ____________

From the following information, answer the questions.

The village of Ashley is due north of Calne and due east of the village of Bourne which, in turn, is due north of Dalton. The four villages make the corners of a square.

17 Which village is west of Ashley? ____________

18 Which village is south of Bourne? ____________

19 Which direction is Calne from Ashley? ____________

20 Which direction is Calne from Bourne? ____________

Total

TEST 37: Mixed

Test time: 0 5 10 minutes

Change the first word into the last word by changing one letter at a time, and making two new, different words in the middle.

Example CASE CASH WASH WISH

1	PLAN	______	______	STAY
2	TYPE	______	______	SORE
3	CLIP	______	______	CROW
4	SOUL	______	______	FOOT

Which one letter can be added to the front of all of these words to make new words?

Example care cat crate call clip

5	__rain	__lend	__rake	__east	__and
6	__end	__out	__ever	__earn	__awful
7	__scent	__maze	__wake	__shore	__jar
8	__lad	__orge	__amble	__listen	__range

A B C D E F G H I J K L M N O P Q R S T U V W X Y Z

Fill in the missing symbols, letters or numbers, or underline the words.

Example AB is to CD as PQ is to RS.

9 AZ is to FU as HS is to _____.

10 ZBE is to GIL as NPS is to _____.

11 Butterfly is to nectar as (pillowcase, caterpillar, lion) is to (bed, leaf, pillow).

12 Slow is to tortoise as (flat, brush, fast) is to (hedgehog, pancake, hare).

13 T17 is to Q20 as L25 is to _____.

14 ?!£% is to %£!? as @$/; is to _____.

15 Bow is to arrow as (dart, gun, target) is to (bullet, gun, target).

16 Speed is to speedometer as (time, race, supersonic) is to (clock, car, jet).

Find and underline the two words that need to change places for each sentence to make sense.

Example She went to letter the write.

17 Guinea-pigs feeds her Sally every day before breakfast.

18 For lunch today we had roast salad followed by fruit chicken.

19 I am maths my finding homework hard.

20 My favourite starts programme television at 8.00pm.

Total

Test 38: Mixed

Test time: 0 5 10 minutes

Change the first word of the third pair in the same way as the other pairs to give a new word.

Example bind, hind bare, hare but, hut

1	quiz, quite	flux, flute	plan, ______
2	practice, price	stopping, sting	pleasant, ______
3	pat, pout	flat, flout	rat, ______
4	sludge, slug	fudge, fug	budge, ______
5	frame, blame	fright, blight	frown, ______

Look at the pair of words on the left. Underline the one word in the brackets that goes with the word outside the brackets in the same way as the first two words go together.

Example good, better bad, (naughty, worst, worse, nasty)

6	short, tall	wide, (empty, fat, broad, narrow)
7	through, around	under, (beneath, over, next, by)
8	chatter, babble	talk, (quiet, silent, speak, noise)
9	delicate, flimsy	light, (illuminate, heavy, darken, substantial)
10	laces, tie	button, (chocolate, fasten, trousers, nose)

A B C D E F G H I J K L M N O P Q R S T U V W X Y Z

Give the two missing groups of letters and numbers in the following sequences. The alphabet has been written out to help you.

11	45	16	____	20	35	____	30	28	
12	4	8	7	____	____	14	13	17	
13	p4	q6	r9	s13	____	u24	____	w39	
14	ACZ	BDY	CEX	DFW	EGV	FHU	____	____	
15	ADb	____	ILj	MPn	QTr	UXv	YBz	____	GJh

Look at the first group of three words. The word in the middle has been made from the two other words. Complete the second group of three words in the same way, making a new word in the middle of the group.

Example PAIN INTO TOOK ALSO SOON ONLY

16	SPOT	TOAD	RAID	BOOM	______	SALT
17	CATS	STAB	BILE	BIRD	______	PINK
18	TRIP	PINT	PANT	FEAR	______	GRID
19	SLOW	WOOL	POSH	SLAT	______	KILL
20	TEAM	MEAT	MILE	LEAF	______	DICE

Total

TEST 39: **Mixed**

Test time: 0 5 10 minutes

From the information supplied, answer the questions.

Naomi, Fern, Husna and Debra are friends at secondary school.

Fern, Naomi and Husna learn Spanish.
Naomi, Husna and Debra study Art.
Husna learns Greek.
Debra and Naomi do Textiles.

Husna, Fern and Debra study French.
Debra, Fern and Naomi do Chemistry.
Fern and Debra do Geography.
Fern and Husna do Music.

1 Who does French but does not do Art? ____________

2 Who does Chemistry but not Geography? ____________

3 Who does Art and Spanish but not Geography or Textiles? ____________

4 Who does not study Music, Greek or Spanish? ____________

5 Who does the fewest subjects? ____________

A B C D E F G H I J K L M N O P Q R S T U V W X Y Z

The code for the word CANDLE is ECPFNG. Using the same code:

encode these words.

6 LIGHT ____________ 7 DARKNESS ____________

decode these words.

8 NWEMA ____________ 9 ETCBA ____________

Complete the following sentences in the best way by choosing one word from each set of brackets.

Example Tall is to (tree, <u>short</u>, colour) as narrow is to (thin, white, <u>wide</u>).

10 Solid is to (jelly, fluid, rigid) as strong is to (liquid, weak, sturdy).

11 Thrash is to (scold, burn, defeat) as crush is to (conquer, draw, defy).

12 Accurate is to (inaccurate, straight, clever) as true is to (real, genuine, false).

13 Hard is to (possible, firm, slim) as coarse is to (dinner, harsh, smooth).

14 Modest is to (fashionable, proud, shut) as humble is to (meek, arrogant, lowly).

Write the following letters or words in alphabetical order.

15 DRAUGHT ____________ 16 COMPUTER ____________

17 DREAM DRAWN DRAWL ____________

18 HEARTH HEATER HEARTY ____________

19 In alphabetical order, which day of the week comes after Monday? ____________

From the information supplied, answer the question.

I appear twice in INCORRUPTIBLE, once in RIDDLE and not at all in PENCIL.

20 Which letter is being described? ____

Total

Test 40: Mixed

Test time: 0 5 10 minutes

A B C D E F G H I J K L M N O P Q R S T U V W X Y Z

Give the two missing groups of letters and numbers in the following sequences. The alphabet has been written out to help you.

Example	CQ	DP	EQ	FP	GQ	HP		
1	6	15	___	___	18	9	24	6
2	___	___	XCD	WDE	VEF	UFG	TGH	SHI
3	60h	50g	41f	33e	26d	20c	___	___
4	BCa	FGe	JKi	NOm	___	VWu	___	DEc

Change the first word into the last word by changing one letter at a time, and making two new, different words in the middle.

Example CASE CASH WASH WISH

5	WOOD	______	______	WARE	**6**	NOSE	______	______	RICE
7	LAZY	______	______	TAME	**8**	MICE	______	______	RISK
9	PYRE	______	______	SURF	**10**	BEST	______	______	GOAT
11	PLEA	______	______	FLOW	**12**	COME	______	______	HOST

Which one letter can be added to the front of all of the words to make new words?

Example	care	cat	crate	call	clip
13	__heel	__hat	__all	__hale	__eighty
14	__eight	__erring	__eel	__edge	__earth
15	__otter	__ark	__light	__honey	__rattle
16	__lope	__at	__bony	__state	__vent

Eight people went to the theatre. The numbered seats are the ones they have tickets for. Using the information below, work out where each person sat.

Judy sat next to her sister.
Clement sat next to Pravin.
Gretel sat right at the side of the theatre.
Harold sat nearer Kang than anyone else.
Kang sat to the left of Harold.
Sandra sat directly three rows behind Pravin.
Penelope sat diagonally in front of Sandra.

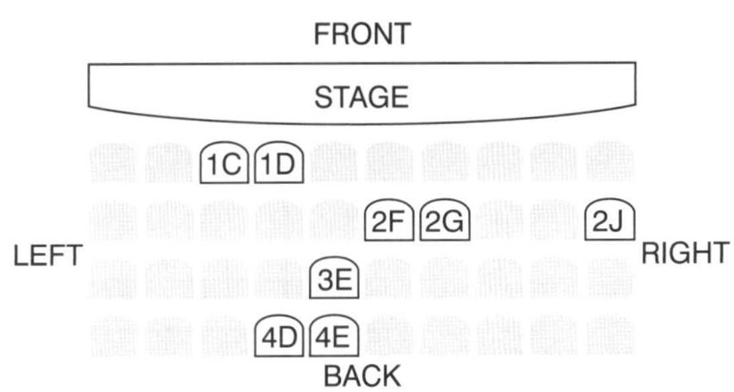

17–20 1C = ____________ 1D = ____________

2F = ____________ 2G = ____________ 2J = ____________

3E = ____________ 4D = ____________ 4E = ____________

Time for a break! Go to Puzzle Page 46

Total

Puzzle 1

Take the words and place them in the grid so that each word reads horizontally and vertically.

Example

EVERY
BREAD
DOYEN

B	R	E	A	D
R		V		O
E	V	E	R	Y
A		R		E
D	O	Y	E	N

1

INLET
PRIZE
ENTER

2

ENDED
ACRID
AWARE

3

SALTS
STRAP
LIVER

4

NEEDS
TAUPE
BATON

5

MEAT THEN
ACHE EACH

6

AUNT DAIS
STOP INTO

7

AREA RARE
PRAY YEAR

8

NAME SIGN
GERM IDEA

9

ALONE
EAGER
GOUDA
ENDED
READS

10

MEANT
PESTO
THREE
AREAS
STAMP

Puzzle 2

Help Freddy to jump from one lily-pad to the next by changing one letter at a time. Watch out! The clues have been mixed up!

Example

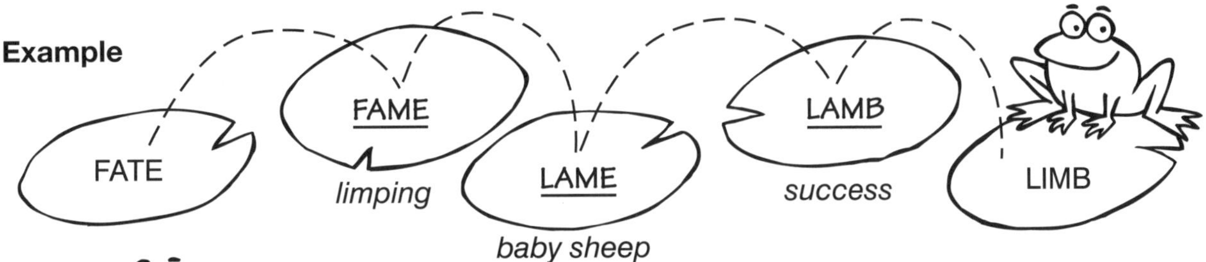

1

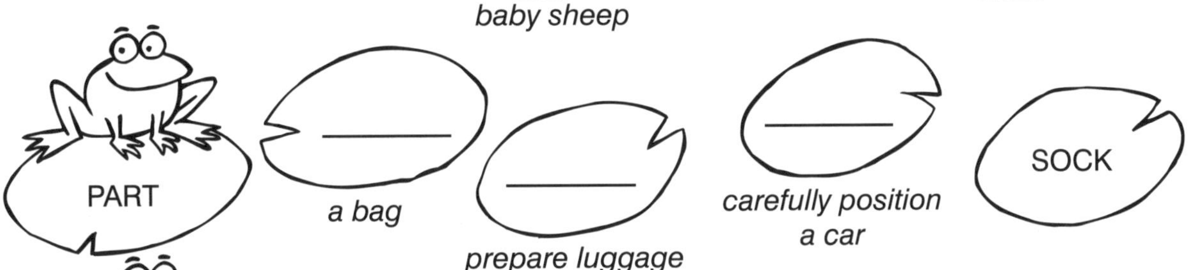

2

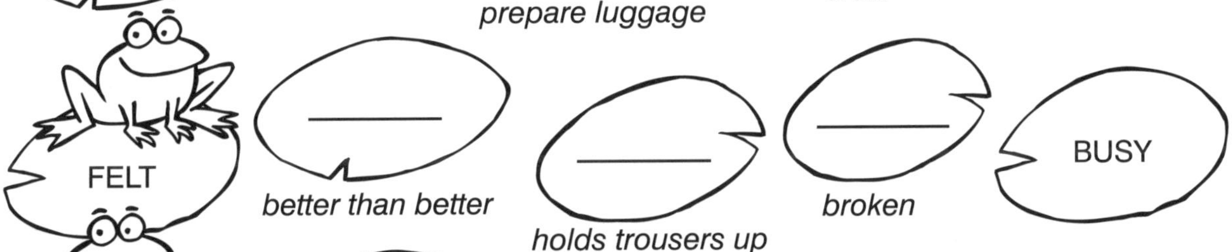

3

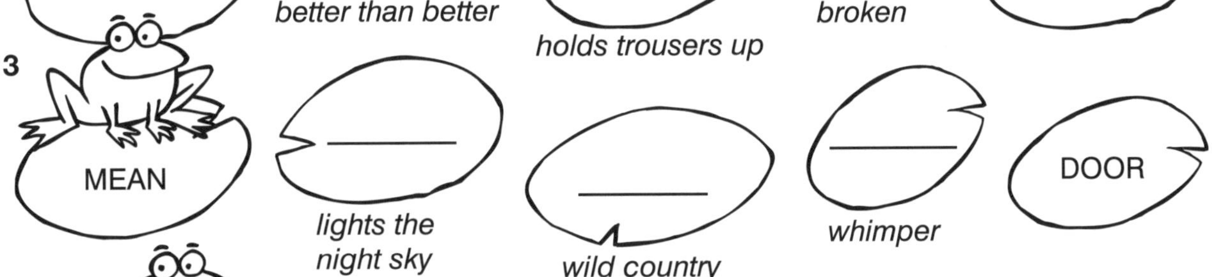

4

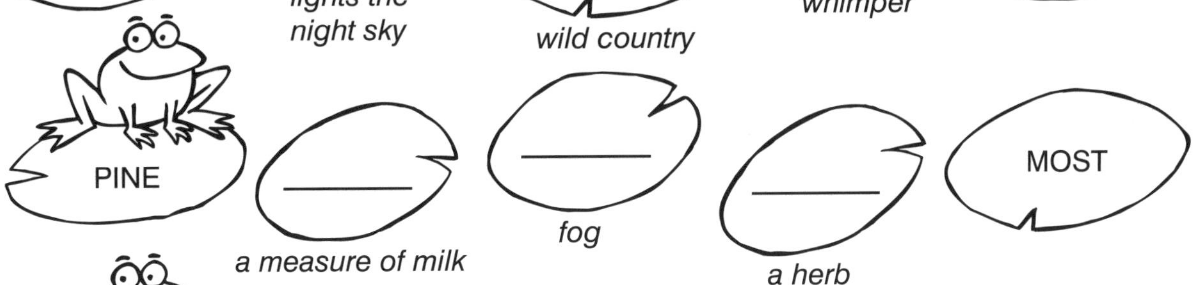

5

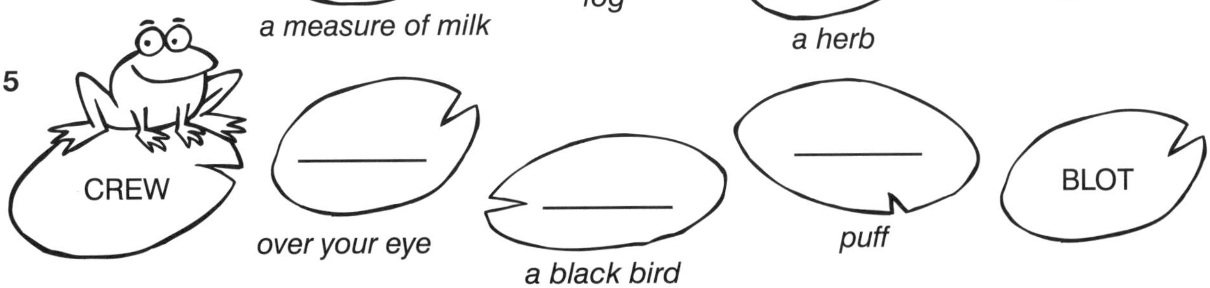

Puzzle 3

Lucy, Clare, James and Jamila were all taken to Blackpool for a day trip over the summer holidays. Each of them was taken by an older relative. In the afternoon, before they went home, they were allowed one last treat.

From the information below, and using the grid to help you, work out which relative was with each child and what treat each of them chose. Fill in the table at the bottom of the page when you have worked it all out.

	mum	grandpa	aunt	sister	funfair	donkey ride	ice cream	beach games
Lucy								
Clare								
James		✗						
Jamila								
funfair								
donkey ride								
ice cream								
beach games								

Grandpa sat in a deck-chair while his granddaughter had a donkey ride.
Jamila was frightened of donkeys and did not want to go near them.
Clare was hungry and bought an ice cream with a female relative.
James and his big sister decided not to play beach games.
Mum had great fun playing beach games with her child.

	RELATIVE	TREAT
Lucy		
Clare		
James		
Jamila		

Puzzle 4

In the sets of words below, there is a word that links all the other words together. This word reads vertically down the lightly shaded column of each grid. The first one has been started for you. Place all the words into each grid and then read down the lightly shaded column to find your linking word.

	S	N	O	W	F	L	A	K	E

FLOWER BATHROOM BARGE SEASIDE SNOWFLAKE

1 The linking word is: ____________________

TEETH DINNER MUNCHING ROAST GRAVY VEGETABLE

2 The linking word is: ____________________

PRISON COMMA ARTICLE ADJECTIVE STORY
QUESTION SUBJECT LETTER

3 The linking word is: ____________________

Puzzle 5

Using the letters in the star, make as many words as you can. You must use the central letter every time and each letter only once. No two-letter words, initials or proper nouns are allowed. Good luck!

Example

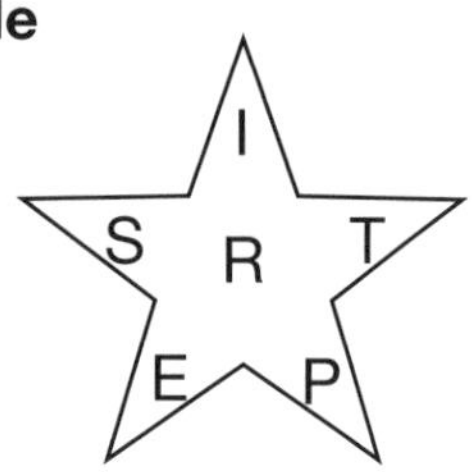

priest	strip	ripe	sir
sprite		tire	rip
		rest	

For a good score aim to get: 2 x 6-letter words
8 x 5-letter words
8 x 4-letter words at least!

6-letter words

5-letter words

4-letter words

3-letter words

Progress Grid

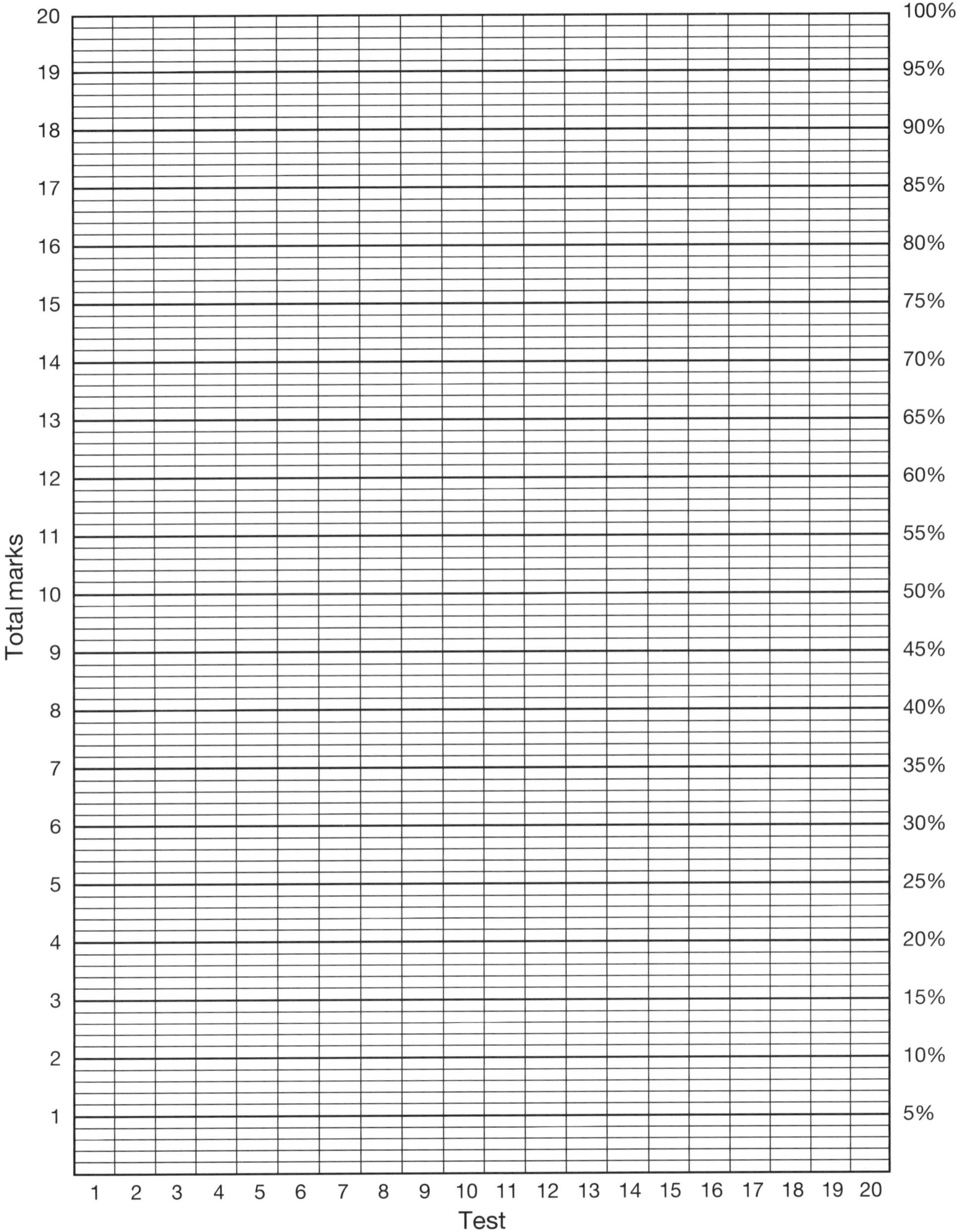

Progress Grid

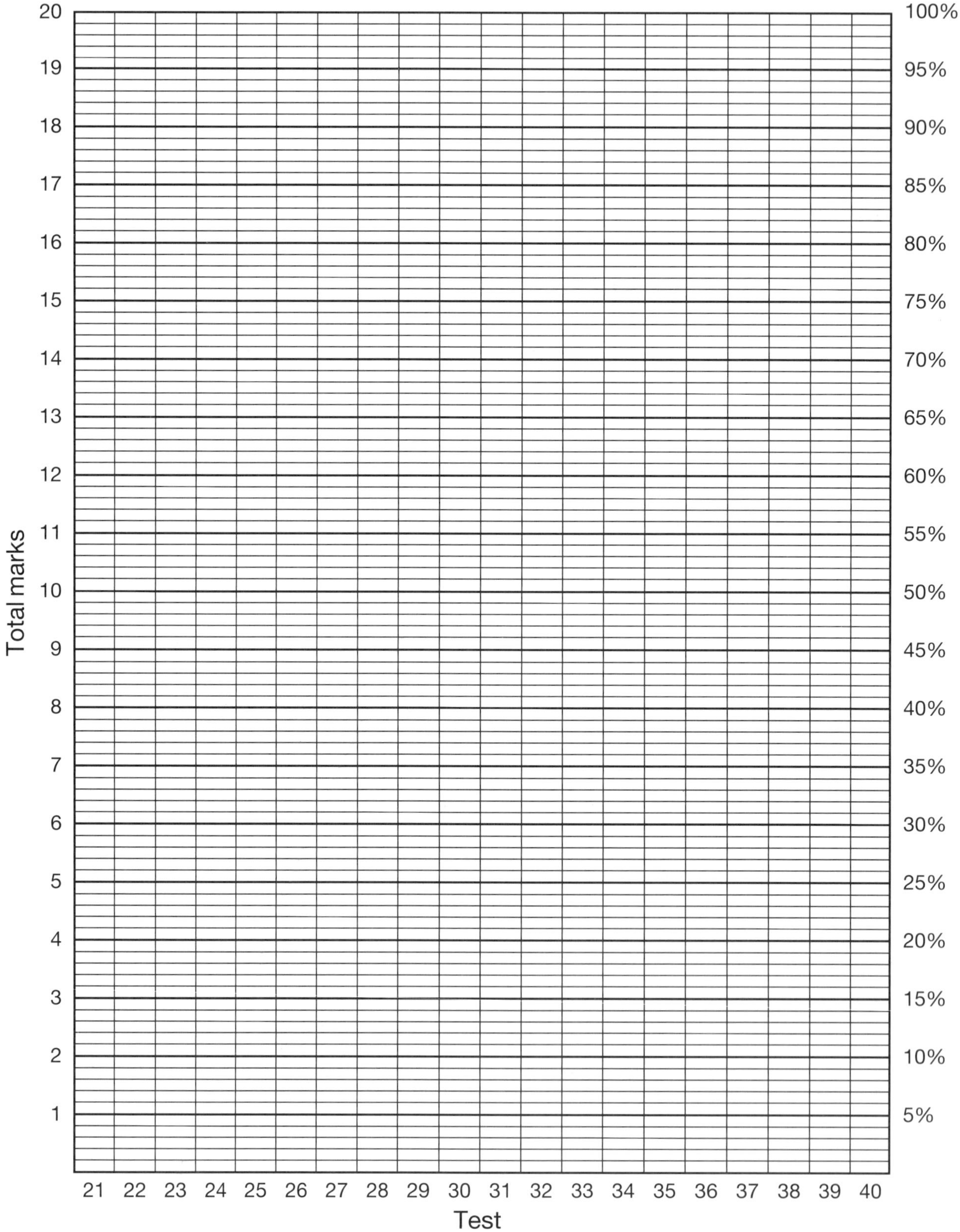